To Eliza
w/love!

2006

To Liza
Keep cookin

2006

The Lady & Sons Just Desserts

MORE THAN 120 SWEET TEMPTATIONS
FROM SAVANNAH'S FAVORITE RESTAURANT

PAULA H. DEEN

PHOTOGRAPHS BY ALAN RICHARDSON

SIMON & SCHUSTER
NEW YORK · LONDON · TORONTO · SYDNEY

SIMON & SCHUSTER
Rockefeller Center
1230 Avenue of the Americas
New York, NY 10020

SIMON & SCHUSTER and colophon are
registered trademarks of Simon & Schuster, Inc.

For information about special discounts for bulk purchases,
please contact Simon & Schuster Special Sales:
1-800-456-6798 or business@simonandschuster.com

DESIGNED BY KEVIN HANEK
ILLUSTRATIONS BY RENÉE HERMAN
PHOTOGRAPHER: ALAN RICHARDSON
PHOTOGRAPHER'S ASSISTANTS: LEVI BROWN, PAUL SIRISALEE
FOOD STYLIST: MICHAEL PEDERSEN
ASSISTANT FOOD STYLIST: JUDI ORLICK
PROP STYLIST: DEBRAH E. DONAHUE
PROP STYLIST'S ASSISTANT: STEPHANIE MAIE

Manufactured in the United States of America

3   5   7   9   10   8   6   4   2

Library of Congress Cataloging-in-Publication Data
Deen, Paula H.
The Lady & Sons just desserts : more than 120 sweet temptations
from Savannah's favorite restaurant / Paula H. Deen
p. cm.
1. Desserts.   2. Cookery, American—Southern Style.   3. Ladies & Sons (Restaurant)
I. Title: Lady and Sons just desserts.   II. Title.
TX773 .D2966 2002
641.5975—dc21   2002017006
ISBN-13: 978-0-7432-9020-3
ISBN-10: 0-7432-9020-8

This work is dedicated to the memory of my wonderful parents,
the late Earl W. Hiers, Sr., and Corrie Paul Hiers.
For without them, nothing would have been possible.
This is truly sweets for the sweet.

Acknowledgments

WITHOUT THE LOVE AND SUPPORT of a lot of people this project would not have been possible. My brother, Bubba, and sons Jamie and Bobby—along with the entire staff at The Lady & Sons—allowed me to leave the restaurant to give birth to this book. They all rose to the top like the finest cream. Thank you all so much for being the people that y'all are. I love each and every one of you so much.

A warm thanks goes out to the hundreds of thousands of y'all who have graced us with your presence at The Lady & Sons. I've had the privilege of personally meeting so many of you. Y'all are so sweet with your thanks for the food we so lovingly prepare for you, and some of you come bearing recipes, offering to share with us your family traditions and memories. A heartfelt acknowledgment goes out to y'all: Sybil Barnett; Carol Berendt; Douglas Boyce; Lynn Boyter; Lauren Burke; Bob and Julia Christian; Captain Judy Helmey; Clary's; LeAnn Coleman; Sandra Cowan; Carolyn Cundiff; Joan Duke; Susan Dupuy; Lynn Ekfelt; Beth English; Paulette Faber; June Foster; Damon Fowler; Nancy Girard; Jane Gottschalk; Gabriel's Desserts; Johnnie Gabriel; The Gastonian; The Granite Steps; Marvin Hamlisch; Shaun Hawkins; Beth Hiers; Laura Holland; Brenda Hollis; Theresa Jaworski; Sean Jones; Olivia Lanier; Ludovic Lefebvre; Marge Maddox; Jackie Mullins; Donna Pickard; Nancy Skains; Pam Strickland; Rachel Strickland; River Street Sweets; Nan Tatum; and Robin Wilson.

I can't put into words the way I feel about my editor, Sydny Miner. She showed the most wonderful care and consideration in that kind Sydny way. My publicity director, Ginger Barton, also a Georgia girl, has worked tirelessly on my behalf. Jeanne Strongin, the photographer who was able to capture the handsomeness of my sons Jamie and Bobby, even took an old woman and made her look not half bad. To Jackie Seow, the art director, and Kevin Hanek, the book designer, thanks goes to both of y'all for your enthusiastic support and efforts on behalf of this project.

A million thanks goes to Jonathon Brodman, copy editing supervisor, and to Virginia McRae, my copy editor, who had to learn how to speak southern.

Thank you, thank you, thank you: to my cousin Don Hiers, who sat patiently and lovingly by my side at the computer for many hours, and challenged me to do my best.

And last but not least, to my personal agent, Barry Weiner, along with Lydia Wills, my literary agent; Barry, how lucky I am to have someone who has never quit believing in me.

Contents

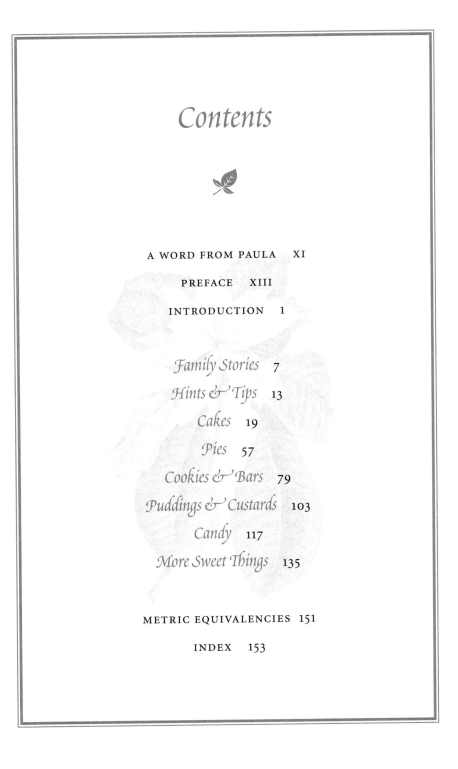

A Word from Paula

HEY, FRIENDS, IT SEEMS LIKE JUST YESTERDAY that I was writing the preface for this wonderful little book. *The Lady & Sons Just Desserts* has a very special place in my heart because it represents the huge change that took place in my life while it was being written. Could it really have been four years since my dogs Otis and Sam ran away from me and straight into Michael Groover's arms? Little did I know that Sam and Otis had such great taste! With no effort they found the man who would become my husband and my best friend. How appropriate that I was finishing up a dessert book when I met the best dessert a girl could hope to have! So I think y'all can understand why this book holds such sentimental value for me. Not only are the recipes wonderful, but now I have someone to serve them up to.

All my new books are in hardcover with wonderful color photographs of some of my favorite recipes. While the spiral-bound format does have some pluses, nothing can take the place of a hardcover book. With care hardcovers can literally last forever, and I'm so happy that *The Lady & Sons Just Desserts* will now fall into that category. Hopefully this book and my marriage will last forever!

I do know that a lot of the recipes in this book you'll want in your files for the rest of your life. One recipe that you don't want to miss is Not Yo' Mama's Banana Pudding! No matter where I go, from California to New York, someone always comes up and hugs and thanks me for sharing this great little recipe. The Blueberry Dumplin's, Gooey Butter Cakes, Pecan Dreams, Key Lime Grits Pie, Jamie's Coconut Cake, Bobby's Caramel Cake, and the Pine Bark candy all received great reviews, which really warms my heart because a recipe is no good if it works only for me. I hope that for those of you using this book for the first time you will love it has much as others and myself do. For those of you who have enjoyed *The Lady & Sons Just Desserts* in its original form I hope will be as thrilled as I am to now have it in a long-lasting hardcover.

As always I send you love and best dishes, from my kitchen to yours,
Paula Deen

Preface

Just Desserts, Kinda, Sorta, Not Really

THIS BOOK IS ABOUT *Just Desserts,* and this story is about Just Desserts, kinda, sorta. You know, I just can't *stand* the thought of folks coming into The Lady & Sons and going away hungry, so we do everything we can to make sure they're happy and full when they leave. Well, on a recent warm summer afternoon, that was definitely not a problem with one couple. The story I'm about to tell you is true, cross my heart and hope to die!

Our guests were from the West Coast; it had been a year since their last visit to the restaurant, and they were starving for our southern cookin'. But I tell y'all what, if everybody enjoyed our food as much as this couple I'd be outta business! Don't get me wrong, we're so glad to see 'em, but ain't we glad it's just once a year!!!

Because before this couple left, they had eaten twenty-four pieces of chicken. You heard me right, that's three chickens, folks. And this couple didn't weigh 250 pounds between the two of them. Ooh, if only I could eat that way and look that good!

Okay. So if that's all they ate, it's not *that* much. But when you kick in the other three plates of vegetables they had apiece, *that's* a pile of food. Oh, and did I forget to tell you she also ate four cheese biscuits and six hoecakes?

So now here we are, finally, to *Just Desserts.*

At the end of your meal, our servers pass through the room, stopping at each table with a tray of wonderful desserts. You might find banana pudding (or Marvin's Banana Cream Pie, page 110), hot peach cobbler, gooey butter cake, lemon curd pudding, or pecan dreams, to name a few. So you see, you really do need to remember to save a little room for dessert. Well, this gentleman forgot to do that. He immediately refused, saying he couldn't possibly eat another bite, and she leaned her cute little self across the table and whispered, "Choose the pound cake, dear," then turned to the server and said with a sweet smile, "and I'll have the peach cobbler." She ate both of 'em.

Now, I want y'all to understand something. Neither my staff nor myself usually notices the quantity of food our guests eat. But when you have someone who enjoys the quality *and* the quantity of our food as much as this couple did, you can't help but take notice and relish their enjoyment.

In fact, I think the lady summed it up best when she said, "You know, we anticipate going back to re-experience something wonderful, and oftentimes it's not what we've remembered and we wind up only being disappointed."

And with this, she looked up at the server and said, "But not here."

Introduction

HAVE YOU EVER BEEN SICK and tired of being sick and tired? Well, this was the position I found myself in in 1989. I wanted to be able to act instead of react. I wanted to make choices for myself instead of taking what came my way through the actions of others. I wanted to be my own woman.

Back in 1965, after I had graduated from high school, my daddy—so badly—wanted to send me to school in Florida to study to be a dental hygienist. Yuck! I had just finished the most cram-filled fun social three years of my life at Albany High School and now I was supposed to be a dental hygienist? It was obvious a mad coon had bitten my daddy.

"I'm sorry, Daddy," I said, "I just can't bear the thought of spending the rest of my life smelling people's stinky breath. *But,*" I went on to say, "how about the Patricia Stevens Modeling School."

"Absolutely not!" he said. "I will not turn my eighteen-year-old daughter loose in Atlanta."

Since we couldn't agree on the education thing, *I* would just solve all the problems by marrying my high school sweetheart.

One night my mother slipped into my bedroom and sat on the side of my bed. The look on her face was sad and full of concern as opposed to the soft sweet smile she normally wore. "Paula, I want you to give careful consideration to the decision you've made, because this commitment should be for a lifetime. If there's anything that bothers you at all about the young man that you have planned to marry make sure it's something you can live with, because contrary to what you may think you don't have the ability to change people."

Well, I just couldn't believe it. My daddy wants me to be a dental hygienist and my mother is suggesting that my marriage might not be a perfect one. Of course, my fiancé *was* perfect, and I was going to be the perfect wife and mother.

So the wedding was held, and I think it took me all of three months to realize I would have made the perfect dental hygienist!

The dreams of a perfect life were shattered seven months after my wedding. My daddy died.

How could this charismatic, wonderful, forty-year-old man whom we all depended on be gone from us forever? The pain this brought to our family was devastating, and I thought that things could get no worse. But four years later my beautiful mother died. She was forty-four years old.

Besides myself, Mother left behind a sixteen-year-old son, my little brother, whom I adored. By this time I also had two little boys of my own under the age of three. The pain I felt for myself was riveting, but the pain I felt for my brother, Bubba, can't even be put into words. I have searched for them, but cannot find them. So, at the ripe old age of twenty-three I had the responsibility of raising two babies, and trying to continue the job that my mother had started with one of her babies. And don't forget the husband.

Over the years, I began to have symptoms of agoraphobia. At one point, I wondered if I would ever be able to leave my home again. Panic attacks became a way of life. I was at my lowest when I knew I could no longer leave the house to accompany my children to the activities they loved. If my boys couldn't walk, they didn't go.

So in spite of the deep love I had for my family, I found I was not the perfect mother. I was not the perfect wife. And I didn't have the perfect husband.

When I was forty, my husband announced that he was accepting a position in Savannah, Georgia. I had to leave behind everything that I knew and loved. I was barely able to function in the town in which I had been born and lived my whole life. How was I ever going to function in a strange new city on the other side of the state?

Well, after arriving in Savannah I handled the move by going to bed for two months. There seemed to be no end to the tears. I had to get out of bed to eat, but I did not have to get out of bed to cry. Albany, my home town, might as well have been two thousand miles away rather than two hundred, and because I couldn't make the journey back home alone, I was stuck.

Then one day I woke up and it was like turning on a light switch and I could see clearly. I decided at that moment I was going to get out of that bed and begin living life to the fullest.

I decided at that moment I would no longer let the fear of fear control my life, and I spent the next two years pondering how I could improve my life and the lives of my children. I wanted so much to give my sons wings either through education or a business, something that they could sink their teeth into. So in 1989, I finally made the decision to follow in my Grandmother Paul's footsteps.

My Granddaddy and Grandmama Paul were in the restaurant and lodging business. Granddaddy Paul knew he had a jewel in my grandmother because she was a fabulous southern cook. Grandma and I spent many years in the kitchen together, her teaching, me watching and learning, laughing together, and enjoying the fruits of our labor. I now realize that I was getting an education without going to school.

I'll never forget my grandmother's words the day I called to let her know what I had decided to do. I rattled on quickly, and when I finally ran out of breath and became quiet there was just silence on the other end. Just when I thought our call must have been disconnected my grandmother said, "Paula. Have you lost your damned mind!"

I busted out laughing, "Well, Grandmama, the apple doesn't fall far from the tree, does it?"

So at the age of forty-two, I turned to my stove and began a business called The Bag Lady. The sum total of my starting capital was two hundred dollars. I spent fifty dollars on groceries, about forty dollars on a cooler, and the rest on a business license and incidentals. This girl was off and running!

It was just a good thing that I didn't know how far and how long I was gonna have to run, 'cause I might not have made it if I'd known how long the track was. It wasn't unusual for me to work a sixteen- or twenty-hour day. I prepared fresh meals daily for people who were stuck in their offices and to be delivered by my sons, Jamie, twenty-one, and Bobby, eighteen, and their girlfriends.

While my children were running their daily routes I cleaned the kitchen from top to bottom and then immediately began the next day's preparations. It was a never-ending cycle, but determination would not allow me to tire of it.

Before I knew it, two years had passed, and I found myself moving into a bona fide restaurant space in the Best Western Central hotel on the south side of Savannah. I would remain there for five years, and I found out that running The Bag Lady was like a day in the park compared to running a full-service restaurant.

My hours were governed by the Best Western's policies, which required me to serve three meals a day, seven days a week. And I continued to maintain The Bag Lady. I decided that the restaurant would be named The Lady, hoping people would associate The Lady with The Bag Lady and bring us instant credibility.

The lack of revenue would require all the work to be done by my sons, their girlfriends, and me. Thank God for those two pretty girls! They were wonderful on the dining room floor. Before we knew it we'd made lots of friends and were serving many Southside business people. My newfound independence brought along the ability to ask for the inevitable. My marriage of twenty-seven years was finally over.

Now that I had settled my personal life, my every thought was about my next business move. My cooking style was southern plantation cuisine, reminiscent of the Old South. Downtown historic Savannah was the place for me.

I'll be forever grateful to Michael Brown. A downtown developer, one day he walked into The Lady and informed me that he had the perfect location for us. We met on the corner of Congress and Montgomery streets. As we leaned against an old building and chatted, Michael pointed across the street to the old Barnett's Educational Supply Building. It *was* perfect. That afternoon, Michael and I consummated the deal with a handshake. Talk about naive! I had just committed myself to a twelve-year lease in an old building that would require $150,000 worth of work.

Being turned down time after time by different financial institutions almost discouraged me. But my passion would not allow me to quit, and I was determined not to stop until someone listened and would agree to help me. Doug McCoy, a local banker, was the man who finally listened.

He felt that I could make it, but that I still didn't have enough collateral in spite of the money I'd managed to save.

A couple of local businessmen had spoken with me about the possibility of backing me, but I really wasn't looking for a partner. Just when I thought I might have to seriously reconsider that prospect, my Aunt Peggy and Uncle George stepped forward and agreed to put up a certificate of deposit as my collateral.

How does one thank someone for giving them a new start on life? I'll forever be grateful to my Aunt Peggy and Uncle George.

We still had many obstacles to overcome—the biggest one being almost a year of downtime with no income except what my catering brought in. As construction dragged on I became poorer with each passing day. I'll never forget one day my younger son, Bobby said, "Mama, I'm hungry but I don't have any money."

I said, "Well, son, I've got one more little change box. Let's go back here and see how much is in it."

As I was sifting through the coins I got a glimpse of something green hidden down in the bottom of that box. It was a fifty-dollar bill! Bobby and I stood there and laughed our heads off and quickly headed to McDonald's and ordered two number threes!

Opening day, January 8, 1996. We opened to the public with not one but *two* overdrawn accounts. My sons and I were full of apprehension, but we were dedicated to serving the best meal to our guests we were capable of preparing.

I'll never forget that day. How our old guests from the Best Western knew we were open I'll never know since we couldn't afford advertising. But they showed up, and I spent that lunch shift crying and hugging everybody's neck and thanking them for not forgetting us. This business was truly built for and by my Savannah friends.

It wasn't long before our guest list grew to include people from all parts of the world. And they all seemed to have one thing in common—they loved cheese biscuits, hoecakes, fried chicken, and collard greens. I saved up enough money to self-publish my cookbook. Can you imagine my surprise when on its second week's birthday my book was bought by a big publishing house and became *The Lady & Sons Savannah Country Cookbook,* followed in two short years by a second cookbook, *The Lady & Sons, Too!*

The Lady & Sons restaurant quickly became a destination for residents and tourists alike. One of these people was Jerry Shriver, food critic with *USA Today.* He and his guests were so cute, smiling and gobbling everything down we brought to them. I knew he enjoyed it, but I had no idea he enjoyed it enough to honor it as the "Most Memorable Meal" for 1999, in the December 19 issue of *USA Today,* putting us number one over restaurants in places like Paris, New York City, and Chicago! Thank you, Jerry. What a difference you made in my life!

I have a dear friend in Savannah named Carol Perkins, who moved to Savannah from New York City, where she had lived a very full and exciting life as a Victoria's Secret model. During her years in New York, Carol met Gordon Elliott, a TV personality on the Food Network, and told him she wanted him to meet me. Well, in walks Gordon, and we hit it off from the start. Before

Gordon left he asked if I would be a guest on his show, "Gordon Elliott's Door Knock Dinners." With some reservations, I accepted.

Before I knew it, Gordy had my sons and me on a plane to Las Vegas. I'll never forget Gordon and me at the craps table until five o'clock in the morning, screaming and cheering!

But we soon had to cut the fun; work called us at 11 A.M. to begin taping an episode of "Door Knock Dinners." After work we were soon back to playtime, enjoying a fabulous meal at Le Cirque.

After dinner Gordon treated us to the fabulous "O" show at the Bellagio, then it was right back to the tables; we didn't leave them again until 8 A.M. the next morning! What a trip, Gordy. A million thanks and much love to you for the good times you showed Jamie, Bobby, and me!

We filmed several other "Door Knock Dinner" episodes. Gordon is directly responsible for introducing me to the Food Network. I've appeared many times on "Ready . . . Set . . . Cook!" with Ainsley Harriott (speaking of great guys, Ainsley's another one of them) and "Food Finds" with Sandra Pinckney, who's also quite a lady.

I'm still enjoying my regular visits to Pennsylvania to appear on the QVC network with recipes from my two previous cookbooks. I have finally arrived at the stage of life that I never dreamed possible for my family or me.

I live in a beautiful home on the water shared with a blue-and-gold macaw, Lady Bird, an umbrella cockatoo named Dixie, a one-eyed cat named Popeye, and two wonderful Shih Tzus, known by the entire neighborhood as Otis and Sam. Toward the end of the writing of this book, Otis and Sam ran over to the computer where I was sitting and started jumping up and down and barking. This was the signal that they had to go potty. As we made our way out the back door on that summer day, it was hotter than a June bride, and definitely not a day I wanted to have to run all over Wilmington Island. Well, the boys immediately pulled a jailbreak, running the opposite of the usual way. They made their way around the big brick wall that surrounds my neighborhood at the edge of the water. Naturally, I'm dressed in old jeans, an old T-shirt, a hat, and sporting no makeup. My book, not my look, was at the top of my priority list.

I chased those dogs around that wall and ran straight into a big burly man I'd never seen, propped on his fence, talking on his cell phone. He bore a strong resemblance to Ernest Hemingway. I quickly apologized for my dogs' invasion of his yard and he just as quickly assured me it was all right. He seemed to be a man that wanted to be left alone even though I heard him mumble, "Let's go have a drink sometime."

Once Otis and Sam tasted that little bit of freedom, they were ready to go back on the other side of the wall. A couple of weeks later it was jailbreak time again. Once again, there stood Ernest Hemingway. This time we made a date to go boating.

Michael Anthony Groover is a fifth-generation Wilmington Island boy with a deep love for his roots and his family. One look at him and you know without a shadow of a doubt that he belongs on the river.

Michael and his world have certainly enriched mine. And his world is his family, his life on the river, his faith, and his ability to care for others. I love the man, I love his family, and I love all that he stands for.

As I sit here completing this introduction, my mind races over the last thirty-five years of my life. It's hard for me to believe that life can be this good. I have learned that I should always keep my head held high and my eyes wide open so that I won't miss the gifts God may have in store for me.

My life is so very full and sweet, surrounded daily in the restaurant by the people that I love so very much: my sons, Jamie and Bobby; my brother, Bubba; my cousin Don; my manager, Lori; my kitchen manager, Rance; my assistant kitchen manager, Aaron; my head cook, Dora; along with Lisa, Charles, and Jelly Roll and our entire restaurant family. Together we all work daily on sharing our food, our traditions, and our love with our guests.

In this cookbook, I hope that y'all enjoy the simple but delicious recipes I've chosen to share with you. I also hope this cookbook will provide a reason for you and your family to come together in the kitchen, forming your own traditions that will make memories that last a lifetime.

Until next time, best dishes from Savannah, Georgia!

Family Stories

Big Sister

EARL W. HIERS, JR.

MY SISTER, who is seven years older than I am, loved to aggravate me, whether we were alone, with a group of her girlfriends, or even in front of Momma and Daddy, it didn't matter. Paula just liked to tease me—her little brother, "Bubba."

Both of our parents had jobs during the late 1950s, so Paula was responsible for looking after me when Momma and Daddy were at work, and they felt comfortable because she was responsible. They knew I was in good hands. Paula smiled every time she had the opportunity to take care of me because it gave her a chance to make me cry like a baby.

When I was about four years old, Paula was taking care of me. Like all little boys—or girls—I wanted to be safe, so if she moved from one room to another I was right behind her. One day she went into her bedroom, pulled out her suitcase and began putting clothes into it.

Being a curious little boy, I asked, "Where are we going?"

"*We* ain't going nowhere," she said. "*I* am."

I stood there with a blank stare on my face, wondering what had I done.

"I'm tired of taking care of you," she said. "You're just a snotty-nosed little brat, and you get on my nerves. You won't leave me alone, and I'm leaving ya."

She swept past me through the bedroom door with her suitcase and stomped down the hallway. "I'm leaving you," she sang. She was *very* happy.

And I was *very* scared.

She flew out the front door and down the steps to the sidewalk. I ran after her and stood on the front porch with tears streaming down my little red cheeks. I'm sure I had no shirt on, no shoes, and probably with no more than a pair of little-boy shorts on. And she was lovin' the moment so much that she turned and even made it to the street, still singing to me, "Bye, Bubba. I'm l-e-a-v-i-n-g!"

And after she'd accomplished what she set out to do, which was to make me cry, she came back and hugged me and said, "I'm not leaving. I'm just teasing you." Of course, I felt very relieved. And although she teased me at every opportunity, I never complained to Momma and Daddy when I had to stay with my sister, because—as a child—I loved her and respected her and looked up to her.

The teasing ended too soon. We lost Momma and Daddy at too young an age, and Paula and I went through many years of trials and tribulations. And we conquered them.

We're still very close today because I have the opportunity to work with my sister at The Lady & Sons. I still love her and respect her with all my heart. And I still look up to her.

Food Is Love

JAMIE DEEN

SOUTHERNERS HAVE ALWAYS used food as a way to express love for one another. I am right this minute twenty pounds over-loved. Down here a new birth warrants a fresh baked pecan pie, the same as the passing of a loved one. If you ever move next door to me, you get a pecan pie. My Great-Grandmother Paul baked them with pecans my brother and I picked up from the yard. We topped that pie with fresh cream that my mom whipped. Bobby and I would dance a jig around the kitchen until she passed down the beaters covered with cream. Mom always said she could just put them away in the drawer, we licked the pair so clean.

Mom learned of her love of cooking the same as us boys: watching, tasting, perfecting the art of soulful southern food. I'm here to tell you, she got it right. After we started our business, more and more people were requesting recipes from her. For five years, she researched family secrets and uncovered a treasure. Looking back on the recipes together was like a family reunion with a family that would be strangers without the legacy of cooking that was a part of them.

For instance, my grandmother always took special care to gently rip the lettuce for her salads so as not to bruise the leaves before adding garden-fresh vegetables and topping it with her Roquefort dressing. I never acquired a taste for the dressing, but always carefully tear my lettuce and give my grandma credit for the technique. I learned my Great-Grandmother Hiers, who was only four foot ten, could still bend over to touch her toes well into her eighties. I also know if you can find a better pound cake than hers you should buy two.

These memories were the joy in developing Mom's first cookbook. Everything else was extremely difficult. Every recipe in the book had to be measured exactly, and exact measuring is not something passed down as easily. A pinch of this, a smidge of that does not translate very well, and the time it took to formulate the measuring was the toughest part of the process. Finally the time had come to take Mom's "third child" to press, but how many to print? The cost of printing is lower if done in high numbers, and after much debate it was decided we would have five thousand made. We figured if nothing else they would make great Christmas gifts for friends and family over the next twenty years.

The print shop is just down the block from the restaurant, so when they called to tell us that the first three were ready to be picked up, we made the walk together. I asked Mom if she was going to cry, and she said she would save the tears for something else. A bet was made and then doubled. Our little family walked in that press shop. The books were passed to us and Mom said with clear eyes, "Pay up."

I smiled and said, "Page four."

Unbeknownst to Mom, Bobby and I had inserted a special tribute of how proud we are of her and the deep love we both feel toward her. Huge tears and deep sobs were mingled in with the joy and laughter we shared together. Mom was so overcome she left work that day and stayed home to read and reread the book cover to cover, over and over again.

Two weeks later a major publishing house from New York called and said they might be interested in purchasing the copyright to publish the book themselves. We were in total shock: Just five years earlier we were working out of our home on a budget that was determined by the sales of the day before. New York and us in the same sentence at that time was like oil and water, but when you start at the bottom there is only one way to go.

At this time our restaurant was doing lunch seven days a week, with private parties Monday through Thursday nights and open to the public on weekend nights. One night, Mom and I were at the restaurant alone, waiting for a group to arrive. The dining room was set and the soft glow of the candles made the scene perfect.

Then the phone rang. It was New York. Mom was a symbol of strength right up to the part when they said congratulations. It was Mom and me in a place that we had helped each other build up from nothing. In that moment when she was laughing and crying and doing her own version of the jig Bobby and I had done years before, I had never been happier. Not for me or the business or the contract or what would become fabulous sales, but for her. All of the hardships that go into starting and running a business were washed away that day and all that remains is . . . love and family.

Bobby's Story

BOBBY DEEN

WE HAVE ARRIVED, and I think I know when it happened. In the spring of 1996, our first year downtown, we felt moderate success, but many nights we had only eight guests for dinner. That comes with the territory of being the new kid on the block. We were trying to find ourselves and compete when what we do best was right under our noses—the southern buffet. If you build it, they will come. And *he* did.

Savannah has become a favorite locale with Hollywood because of all her beautiful natural "eye candy": the moss in the trees, the azaleas in bloom, the squares and history and architecture of our city. We've become accustomed to the cameras and the lights and the film trucks moving into our space, and at times invading our privacy and interrupting our business. In 1996, none of this had affected The Lady & Sons, but it was about to.

Jim Williams of *Midnight in the Garden of Good and Evil* fame had been dead since 1983, but he walked into our restaurant in the spring of 1996 as Kevin Spacey in the character of Jim Williams. He must have enjoyed it, because he came in six or eight times while filming in Savannah. Every time, he sat up front patiently reading his newspaper while he waited for a table. He never tried the buffet; Kevin Spacey is a chicken salad, cold-plate kind of guy.

On the other hand, Josie Wales sidled right up to the buffet and helped himself. It was so surreal to see Clint Eastwood spooning up his own dinner. But a man's gotta eat, and even an icon can fix his own plate.

This man knows how to use his celebrity. He called ten minutes before closing time to make a reservation for ten minutes later. There was one table of three ladies left in the restaurant, and when he walked in—they weren't going anywhere!

After Mr. Eastwood arrived, I slammed the door shut and locked it. It hadn't been busy that night, but all of a sudden people had an urge for coffee and dessert at The Lady & Sons. Not a chance. We were going to enjoy him all to ourselves.

I knew he liked jazz, so I put on John Coltrane's "Soul Trane" CD. I *had* to talk to him. I love his work, and I wanted him to love mine. But the only thing I could think to ask was: "Is the music too loud, Mr. Eastwood?" He looked up at me and said, "No, it's a great CD. Let it play."

We all came to the table after he and his lovely wife, Deana, finished their meal. I still had my foot in my mouth, and I was concerned that my mother might also have a taste for shoe leather. But I shouldn't have given it a thought; she and Mr. Eastwood talked corn bread and rutabagas. He said he hadn't had fresh rutabagas since he was a child, and they brought back memories. And then my mom told him a funny story. At The Lady & Sons we serve hoecake corn bread, fried up in small batches so that it's always fresh. When we start getting low, Mom or a server will yell back to the kitchen, "We need more hoes!" Well, one day Mom stepped into the kitchen and hollered out, "We need more hoes, y'all!" All of a sudden three female kitchen workers were standing in front of Mom. "Here we are," they said. Mom and the whole kitchen staff, along with the three ladies, just doubled over with laughter at their little joke.

He rolled his head back, and with that distinct Clint Eastwood grin, he genuinely laughed. "Wrong kinda hoes, huh?" He enjoyed the food *and* he liked us.

He had a glass of red wine—a Beaujolais to be exact—with those southern rutabagas and corn bread. What a memorable night it was for me and my staff. I can truly say Clint Eastwood "made my day!"

Hints & Tips

In General

- *When in doubt, sift flour before measuring.*

- *When cooking or baking in glass pans, reduce the oven temperature by 25°F.*

- *Oven temperatures (Temperatures can vary. Place an oven thermometer in your oven to make sure it is correct.):*

Slow oven	250° to 325°F	Hot oven	375° to 450°F
Moderate oven	325° to 375°F	Very hot oven	450° to 550°F

- *An average-sized lemon yields about 3 tablespoons juice and 1 tablespoon zest.*

- *An average orange yields a half cup of juice.*

- *To remove nutmeats whole from the shell, soak the nuts overnight in salted water before cracking them.*

- *To peel a coconut, you must drain the milk from it by piercing the "eyes" on the end of the coconut with an ice pick. Place the coconut in an oven until hot to the touch. Remove the coconut and, using a hammer, tap the coconut over its entire surface, particularly at each end. Then place the coconut on a level surface and give it one hard knock and the shell will crack open. Lift the shell off by pieces, peel the brown skin and discard, and cool the nutmeat before grating.*

- *Always use large eggs unless otherwise specified.*

- *Here is a handy table of weights and measures:*

3 teaspoons	=	1 tablespoon	60 drops	=	1 teaspoon
16 tablespoons	=	1 cup	2 cups	=	1 pint
2 tablespoons	=	⅛ cup	2 pints	=	1 quart
4 tablespoons	=	¼ cup	4 quarts	=	1 gallon
5⅓ tablespoons	=	⅓ cup	16 ounces	=	1 pound
12 tablespoons	=	¾ cup	16 liquid ounces	=	1 pint
1 cup	=	½ pint			

Different chocolates may melt differently; it's best to follow the directions on the package. In general, the safe way is to melt in the top of a double boiler (the top pan shouldn't touch the water in the bottom pan) over very low heat. The microwave also works well—just be very careful as the chocolate will burn easily.

You will get a darker, more mellow flavor from the Dutch process versus regular cocoa. Either type can be used in a recipe calling for cocoa.

Homemade vanilla extract: It's so much better than a store-bought extract and wonderfully easy to make: Split 2 vanilla beans lengthwise, then cut them in half crosswise. Put the beans, including any seeds that may fall out, in a clean glass jar. Add ½ cup of bourbon, seal the jar, and give it a vigorous shake. Put in a cool dark cupboard for 2 weeks and shake it well every day. After 2 weeks, let the extract sit undisturbed for 2 more weeks. It is ready to use after that. If you keep replenishing the extract that you use with an equal amount of bourbon, the beans should last you for at least a year, or longer if you use less extract.

Sweetened Condensed Milk

I CAN'T TELL YOU how many times I've started preparing a recipe, only to go to the cabinet and find I have no condensed milk. Hope this helps you out of a possible jam. Oh, by the way, you'll find this to be a good bit cheaper than the store-bought.

This recipe makes the equivalent of one 14-ounce can of sweetened condensed milk.

⅓ cup boiling water

4 tablespoons butter

¾ cup sugar

½ teaspoon pure vanilla extract

1 cup Carnation powdered milk

Using an electric mixer, blend together water, butter, sugar, and vanilla. Add powdered milk and blend until thick. Store in refrigerator for up to a week.

Perfect Measurements

1. When measuring ingredients for desserts, accuracy is of the utmost importance.
2. Never hold measuring spoons over the mixing bowl while measuring. If you accidentally overpour something, such as salt, you could ruin your dish and have to start all over again.
3. When measuring sticky things like syrup, honey, or jelly, spray the measuring cup with a nonstick cooking spray. Almost every drop will come out with ease.
4. Do not use your flatware set (teaspoon or tablespoon) for measuring. Use only proper measuring spoons, except when dropping cookie dough onto baking sheet.

When Whipping Cream:

1. One cup of whipping cream yields 2 cups whipped. Whipping cream and heavy cream are the same. Do not confuse with half-and-half, which *cannot* be whipped.
2. Avoid overbeating, because you will turn whipping cream to butter. You can achieve a stiff peak, but don't take it past that point.
3. I use ¼ cup of sugar to 1 cup whipping cream in most all of my recipes. If this is too sweet for you, simply reduce the amount of sugar to suit your taste.
4. For a different twist, add almond or lemon extracts. Pair the flavors with the appropriate dessert.
5. Try adding cocoa to whipping cream, with a little extra sugar because chocolate is bitter. Simply add cocoa to whipping cream and beat as usual.
6. Be sure your bowl and beaters are well chilled and your cream is very cold.

If You Need to Cut Out Some Fat . . .

1. Frozen vanilla yogurt melted slightly in a microwave makes a great sauce over desserts.
2. You may substitute skim milk for whole with pretty good results. I always use 2% milk.
3. A great substitute for sour cream is nonfat or low-fat plain yogurt. Reduced or nonfat sour cream may not always work for baking unless it's made from cultured or skim milk.
4. Do not substitute low-fat butter, whipped butter, or margarine for butter or regular margarine. There's a good chance you won't like the results.
5. Substitute frozen whipped topping for fresh whipped cream.
6. Lean toward angel food or sponge cake instead of butter cake.

Helpful Hints

1. To ensure an easy roll on jelly-roll cakes, it may be necessary to trim the crisp edges off with a serrated knife. This will prevent the cake from splitting or cracking as you roll it up.
2. Most of the recipe instructions call for greased and floured pans. I use Pam or Baker's Joy, a fat-free cooking spray. If you don't use these, grease your pans with a solid shortening instead of oil.
3. When baking a dense cake such as a pound cake, be careful not to overbeat. This type of cake can actually be beaten by hand if you prefer.
4. There are several ways to determine if a cake is done:

   - When you touch the center with your finger, the cake should spring back.
   - A toothpick, clean broom straw, or metal skewer inserted in the center comes out clean.
   - The cake ever so slightly begins to pull away from the sides of the pan.

5. Try to avoid opening the oven door to peek until the minimum cooking time is up.

6. Allow cakes to cool in the pan 5 to 10 minutes before inverting onto a cooling rack. If you have a stubborn cake, sit the cake pan on a wet, ice-cold dish cloth for a minute or two, invert, and tap a few times on the bottom.

7. To "fix" an overbaked cake, make a simple syrup of equal parts water and sugar along with a teaspoonful of flavoring (lemon, vanilla, maple, coconut, etc.) or a tablespoonful or two of a liqueur (rum or brandy). Bring to a boil, remove from heat, and allow to cool. Pierce cake layers with a fork and brush each with the amount of syrup you think it needs. If this doesn't correct the texture, don't despair—cut the cake up into pieces and use in a trifle recipe.

8. Before baking a layer cake, fill pans, hold 3 or 4 inches from a hard, flat surface, and drop onto the surface several times. This allows air bubbles to escape and helps to produce a more even, level cake.

9. Store the cake in an airtight container. Once the cake has been sliced, you may want to press a piece of waxed paper or tin foil against cut sides to help prevent staling.

10. To prevent those pesty little weevils from hatching in your unused meal or flour, place a few whole bay leaves in the container. Storing unused flour in the freezer or refrigerator will also help prevent their hatching.

11. When you buy flour, transfer it into an airtight container for storage, along with a piece of paper identifying the product. You definitely don't want to confuse your all-purpose flour with the self-rising variety.

12. If recipe calls for "X cups of sifted flour," that means to sift flour before measuring. If it calls for "X cups of flour, sifted," sift the flour after measuring.

13. When buying eggs avoid damaged or cracked ones, as they are rendered useless and may contain bacteria.

14. A pinch of salt added to the sugar when making icings will prevent graining.

Cakes

1-2-3-4 Cakes: *Basic 1-2-3-4 Cake* ✤ *Jamie's Coconut Cake* ✤
Bobby's Caramel Cake ✤ *Six-Layer Chocolate Cake* ✤ *Paula's
Lemon Cheesecake* ✤ Applesauce Cake ✤ Chocolate Cream
Cheese Pound Cake ✤ Brown Sugar Pound Cake ✤ Coconut Pound
Cake ✤ Chocolate Bourbon Pecan Cake ✤ Chocolate Fudge Ribbon
Cake ✤ Cool and Creamy Coconut Cake ✤ Is It Really Better Than
Sex? Cake ✤ Chocolate Sybil Cake ✤ Butter Pecan Cheesecake ✤
Carolyn's Jell-O Cheesecake ✤ Earthquake Cake ✤ Eclair Cake ✤
Fresh Pear Cake ✤ Icebox Fruitcake ✤ Italian Crème Cake ✤
Grandma Paul's Japanese Fruitcake ✤ Orange-Walnut Sunrise
Coffee Cake ✤ Granite Steps Country Blueberry Coffee Cake ✤
Key Lime Mousse Cake ✤ Ludovic's Mom's Chocolate Cake ✤
Mystery Mocha Cake ✤ Old South Jelly Roll Cake ✤ Plum Cake ✤
Savannah Date Nut Cake ✤ Southwest Georgia Pound Cake ✤
Sweet Baby Carrot Cake ✤ Tennessee Banana–Black Walnut Cake
with Caramel Frosting ✤ The Bag Lady's Favorite Chocolate Pound
Cake ✤ Turtle Cake ✤ Wilkes-Barre Cream Cheese Cake ✤
Wilmington Island Marsh Mud Cake

1-2-3-4 Cake

🌿

THIS RECIPE HAS BEEN AROUND since the beginning of time. (It got its name because it uses 1 cup butter, 2 cups sugar, 3 cups flour, and 4 eggs.) Every baker should have the recipe in her file.

My oldest son, Jamie, recently celebrated his thirty-fourth birthday. His girlfriend Stacey, called me and said that the only cake that he liked was "Mama's coconut cake." She asked if I could make it for that night. My favorite coconut cake needs to sit for three days after baking. Since I didn't have this kind of time I decided to make a minor adjustment to the 1-2-3-4 Cake.

Jamie and Bobby were to take their dates for dinner at The Sapphire Grill. I was to hand-deliver the cake at the end of the meal with my best friends, Ann and Susan. The three of us burst into the restaurant singing "Happy Birthday" (loudly and off-key) and carrying the beautiful cake ablaze with candles. The server whisked the cake away and returned with thick slabs of cake. As they lifted their forks to their mouths, I was watching 'em all. As their eyeballs rolled back in their heads, I knew it was going to be a home run. Jamie consumed his slab in four bites!

The recipe for the Basic 1-2-3-4 Cake is followed by several variations: Jamie's Coconut Cake, Bobby's favorite Caramel Cake, Six-Layer Chocolate Cake (which has one of the best fudge frostings you'll ever put in your mouth) and a Lemon Cheese Cake.

Basic 1-2-3-4 Cake

1 cup (2 sticks) butter, at room temperature	3 cups sifted self-rising flour
2 cups sugar	1 cup milk
4 eggs	1 teaspoon pure vanilla extract

Preheat oven to 350°F. Grease and flour three 9-inch cake pans.

Using an electric mixer, cream butter until fluffy. Add sugar and continue to cream well for 6 to 8 minutes. Add eggs, one at a time, beating well after each addition. Add flour and milk alternately to creamed mixture, beginning and ending with flour. Add vanilla and continue to beat until just mixed. Divide batter equally among prepared pans. Level batter in each pan by holding pan 3 or 4 inches above counter, then dropping it flat onto counter. Do this several times to release air bubbles and assure you of a more level cake. Bake for 25 to 30 minutes or until done. Cool in pans 5 to 10 minutes. Invert cakes onto cooling racks. Cool completely and spread cake layers with your favorite frosting to make a 3-layer cake.

SERVES 16 TO 20

Jamie's Coconut Cake

CAKE	FILLING	7-MINUTE FROSTING
1 cup (2 sticks) butter, at room temperature	¾ cup sugar	1½ cups sugar
2 cups sugar	1 cup sour cream	¼ teaspoon cream of tartar or 1 tablespoon white corn syrup
4 eggs	4 tablespoons milk	
3 cups sifted self-rising flour	½ cup flaked, sweetened coconut	⅛ teaspoon salt
		⅓ cup water
1 cup canned, unsweetened coconut milk		2 egg whites
1 teaspoon pure vanilla extract		1½ teaspoons pure vanilla extract
		Flaked, sweetened coconut, for sprinkling

Preheat oven to 350°F. Grease and flour three 9-inch cake pans.

Using an electric mixer, cream butter until fluffy. Add sugar and continue to cream well for 6 to 8 minutes. Add eggs one at a time, beating well after each addition. Add flour and coconut milk alternately to creamed mixture, beginning and ending with flour. Add vanilla and continue to beat until just mixed. Divide batter equally among prepared pans. Level batter in each pan by holding pan 3 or 4 inches above counter, then dropping it flat onto counter. Do this several times to release air bubbles and assure you of a more level cake. Bake for 25 minutes or until golden brown.

While cake is baking, prepare filling. Stir together sugar, sour cream, milk, and coconut in a bowl until well blended. Remove cake layers from oven and allow cake to remain in pans as you prepare to stack and fill. Remove first layer and invert onto cake plate. Using the wrong end of a wooden spoon, poke holes approximately 1 inch apart until entire cake has been poked. Spread one third of filling mixture on cake layer. Top with second layer, repeat process. Top with last layer and repeat process again. (As I stack layers together I stick them with toothpicks to prevent cake from shifting.)

To prepare 7-Minute Frosting, place sugar, cream of tartar or corn syrup, salt, water, and egg whites in the top of a double boiler. Beat with a handheld electric mixer for 1 minute. Place pan over boiling water, being sure that boiling water does not touch the bottom of the top pan. (If this happens, it could cause your frosting to become grainy.) Beat constantly on high speed with electric mixer for 7 minutes. Beat in vanilla and frost top and sides of cake. With additional coconut, sprinkle top and sides of cakes.

SERVES 16 TO 20

Bobby's Caramel Cake

CAKE

1 cup (2 sticks) butter, at room temperature

2 cups granulated sugar

4 eggs

3 cups sifted self-rising flour

1 cup milk

1 teaspoon pure vanilla extract

FILLING

1 cup (2 sticks) butter

2 cups packed light brown sugar

¼ cup milk

1 teaspoon pure vanilla extract

FROSTING

½ cup (1 stick) butter

1 cup packed dark brown sugar

⅓ cup heavy cream, or more as necessary

1 16-ounce box confectioners' sugar

1 teaspoon pure vanilla extract

1 cup chopped nuts (optional)

Preheat oven to 350°F. Grease and flour three 9-inch cake pans.

Using an electric mixer, cream butter until fluffy. Add granulated sugar and continue to cream well for 6 to 8 minutes. Add eggs one at a time, beating well after each addition. Add flour and milk alternately to creamed mixture, beginning and ending with flour. Add vanilla and continue to beat until just mixed. Divide batter equally among prepared pans. Level batter in each pan by holding pan 3 or 4 inches above counter, then dropping it flat onto counter. Do this several times to release air bubbles and assure you of a more level cake. Bake for 25 minutes or until golden brown.

Meanwhile, prepare cake filling. In a saucepan, combine butter, brown sugar, and milk. Cook and stir over medium heat for 3 to 5 minutes. Remove from heat and stir in vanilla.

Remove cake layers from oven and allow cake to remain in pans as you prepare to stack and fill. Remove first layer and invert onto cake plate. Pierce cake layer with a toothpick over entire surface. Spread one third of filling mixture on cake layer. Top with second layer, repeat process. Top with last layer and repeat process again. (As I stack layers together I stick them with toothpicks to prevent cake from shifting.)

To prepare frosting, melt butter in a saucepan over medium heat and stir in brown sugar and cream. Bring to a boil, and transfer to a mixing bowl. Add confectioners' sugar and vanilla. Beat with a handheld electric mixer until it reaches a spreading consistency. At this time it may be necessary to add a tablespoon of heavy cream, or more, if frosting gets too thick. Just be sure to add cream in small amounts because you can always "add to," but you can't take away. Frost cake and sprinkle top with chopped nuts, if desired.

SERVES 16 TO 20

Six-Layer Chocolate Cake

CAKE	FROSTING
1 cup (2 sticks) butter, at room temperature	1 cup granulated sugar
2 cups granulated sugar	⅓ cup cocoa
4 eggs	½ cup (1 stick) butter
3 cups sifted self-rising flour	⅔ cup half-and-half, plus more if needed
1 cup milk	2 tablespoons corn syrup
1 teaspoon pure vanilla extract	⅛ teaspoon salt
	1 16-ounce box confectioners' sugar, sifted, plus 1 cup
	1 teaspoon pure vanilla extract

Preheat oven to 350°F. Grease and flour three 9-inch cake pans.

Using an electric mixer, cream butter until fluffy. Add granulated sugar and continue to cream well for 6 to 8 minutes. Add eggs one at a time, beating well after each addition. Add flour and milk alternately to creamed mixture, beginning and ending with flour. Add vanilla and continue to beat until just mixed. To bake 6 layers, 3 at a time, divide batter in half, then divide one half among prepared pans. Using a spatula, spread batter evenly in pan, then level batter in each pan by holding pan 3 or 4 inches above counter, then dropping it flat onto counter. Do this several times to release air bubbles and assure you of a more level cake. Bake for 15 to 20 minutes or until golden brown. Cool in pans 5 to 10 minutes. Invert cakes onto cooling racks. Cool completely. Repeat process with remaining half of cake batter.

While cakes cool, prepare frosting. Mix granulated sugar, cocoa, butter, half-and-half, corn syrup, and salt in a saucepan, stir, and bring to a full rolling boil. Continue boiling, stirring occasionally, for 3 minutes. (Syrup must become thick and coat spoon, so be sure mixture cooks at a hard rolling boil.) Remove from heat. Beat in confectioners' sugar and vanilla with an electric mixer. Allow frosting to rest for a couple of minutes. At this time, you can determine if it is too thick for spreading. If you need to, add half-and-half, 1 tablespoon at a time, to bring frosting to proper spreading consistency.

SERVES 16 TO 20

Paula's Lemon Cheesecake

LEMON CHEESECAKE *is a very old southern cake that has remained one of the most popular. Even though it doesn't contain any cheese, the filling is very curd-like. Hence the name Lemon Cheesecake.*

CAKE	FILLING
1 cup (2 sticks) butter, at room temperature	8 egg yolks
	1 cup sugar
2 cups sugar	¼ cup (½ stick) butter
4 eggs	Juice and grated zest of 3 lemons
3 cups sifted self-rising flour	
1 cup milk	
1 teaspoon pure vanilla extract	1 recipe 7-Minute Frosting (page 22), without the coconut

Preheat oven to 350°F. Grease and flour three 9-inch cake pans.

Using an electric mixer, cream butter until fluffy. Add sugar and continue to cream well for 6 to 8 minutes. Add eggs one at a time, beating well after each addition. Add flour and milk alternately to creamed mixture, beginning and ending with flour. Add vanilla and continue to beat until just mixed. Divide batter equally among prepared pans. Level batter in each pan by holding pan 3 or 4 inches above counter, then dropping it flat onto counter. Do this several times to release air bubbles and assure you of a more level cake. Bake for 25 to 30 minutes or until golden brown. Cool in pans 5 to 10 minutes. Invert cakes onto cooling racks. Cool completely.

Meanwhile, place filling ingredients in top of double boiler over boiling water (don't let top pan touch the water). Cook and stir until mixture begins to gel or thicken. Remove from heat, allow to cool, and spread between cake layers. Frost top and sides of cake with 7-Minute Frosting, omitting coconut.

SERVES 16 TO 20

Applesauce Cake

This is delicious with a scoop of vanilla ice cream.

1 cup granulated sugar	½ teaspoon salt
½ cup vegetable shortening	1 cup chopped nuts
2 eggs	1 cup raisins
2 cups all-purpose flour	1 cup unsweetened applesauce
1 teaspoon ground cinnamon	Confectioners' sugar, for sprinkling
½ teaspoon ground cloves	
½ teaspoon freshly grated nutmeg	
1 tablespoon baking powder	

Preheat oven to 350°F. Grease a 13 × 9 × 2-inch pan.

Cream together granulated sugar and shortening until fluffy, using an electric mixer. Add eggs, beating well. In another bowl, sift together flour, cinnamon, cloves, nutmeg, baking powder, and salt. Stir nuts and raisins into flour mixture. Add flour mixture and applesauce alternately to creamed mixture, beginning and ending with flour mixture. Pour batter into prepared pan. Bake for 45 minutes or until center of cake is firm to the touch. Sprinkle with confectioners' sugar.

SERVES 16 TO 20

Chocolate Cream Cheese Pound Cake

Rich and delicious.

1 cup (2 sticks) butter, softened	1 teaspoon pure vanilla extract
1 8-ounce package cream cheese, softened	2¼ cups cake flour
	1 teaspoon baking powder
3 cups sugar	¾ cup cocoa
6 eggs	

Preheat oven to 325°F. Grease and flour a 10-inch Bundt pan.

Using an electric mixer, cream together butter, cream cheese, and sugar. Add eggs two at a time, beating well after each addition. Add vanilla. In another bowl, stir together flour, baking powder, and cocoa. Add one half of flour mixture to creamed mixture, beat well, add remaining half of flour mixture, and continue to beat at medium speed for 2 minutes. Pour batter into prepared pan and bake for 1¼ hours. Continue to bake for an additional 15 minutes if necessary, but do not open oven to check cake for at least 1 hour.

CREAM CHEESE POUND CAKE: Replace cocoa with cake flour, making a total of 3 cups flour.

SOUR CREAM POUND CAKE: Substitute 8 ounces sour cream for cream cheese. Add sour cream alternately with the flour. Omit cocoa and use 3 cups cake flour.

CHOCOLATE SOUR CREAM POUND CAKE: Substitute 8 ounces sour cream for cream cheese. Add sour cream alternately with the flour.

SERVES 16 TO 20

Brown Sugar Pound Cake

A SWEET SOUTHERN CLASSIC. You'll need a candy thermometer to make the frosting.

CAKE	FROSTING
1 cup (2 sticks) butter, softened	1 egg, beaten
½ cup shortening	1 cup milk
1 16-ounce box dark brown sugar	3 cups granulated sugar
1 cup granulated sugar	½ cup water
5 eggs	½ cup (1 stick) butter, softened
3½ cups cake flour	1 teaspoon white vinegar
½ teaspoon baking powder	⅛ teaspoon salt
1 cup milk	
1½ teaspoons pure vanilla extract	

Preheat oven to 300°F. Grease and flour a 10-inch Bundt pan.

Using an electric mixer, cream together butter and shortening and add the sugars, 1 cup at a time, continuing to beat. Add eggs one at a time, beating well after each addition. Sift flour and baking powder together in another bowl and add alternately with milk to creamed mixture, beginning and ending with flour mixture. Add vanilla and mix well. Pour batter into prepared pan. Bake for 2 hours.

To prepare frosting, mix together egg and milk and set aside. Place ½ cup of the granulated sugar in a heavy saucepan. Cook over medium-low heat, stirring constantly until melted and brown. Add water and stir until sugar is dissolved. Add remaining 2½ cups granulated sugar and stir into sugar mixture. Add butter, vinegar, and salt. Cook to soft-ball stage (236°F on a candy thermometer), stirring constantly. (A small amount dropped in a glass of water will form a soft ball. If you remove it from the water it will flatten out). Cool to lukewarm. Beat until creamy and spread on cake.

SERVES 18 TO 20

Coconut Pound Cake

¾ cup shortening

1 cup (2 sticks) butter, softened

3 cups sugar

5 eggs

3 cups all-purpose flour

½ teaspoon salt

½ teaspoon baking powder

1 cup milk

2 teaspoons coconut extract

1 3.5-ounce can flaked, sweetened coconut

Preheat oven to 325°F. Grease and flour a 10-inch Bundt pan.

Using an electric mixer, cream shortening, butter, and sugar together. Add eggs one at a time, beating well after each addition. Sift together flour, salt, and baking powder, and add alternately with milk to shortening mixture, beginning and ending with flour. Add coconut extract and stir in coconut. Pour into prepared pan and bake for 1 hour and 25 minutes or until done. Cool for 10 minutes; invert onto cake plate.

SERVES 16 TO 20

Chocolate Bourbon Pecan Cake

THIS IS AN UNFORGETTABLE RECIPE from my cousin's bakery, Gabriel's Desserts. (A ganache is simply a frosting made of chocolate and hot cream.)

FILLING

8½ 1-ounce squares semisweet
   chocolate

½ cup (1 stick) butter

3 jumbo eggs, separated

½ cup sugar

¼ cup bourbon

¼ cup all-purpose flour

1½ cups chopped pecans

GANACHE

1 cup heavy cream

1¼ cups semisweet chocolate
   chips

Preheat oven to 325°F. Grease and flour a 9-inch springform pan.

Melt chocolate and butter in top of a double boiler over slightly simmering water (don't let top pan touch the water). Remove from heat, leaving pot with chocolate over the water; set aside. Whisk egg yolks and half the sugar in a metal mixing bowl, place bowl over slightly simmering water, and whisk while heating to 140°F (yolks will feel warm to the touch). Remove from heat and beat yolk-sugar mixture with an electric mixer to a ribbon stage. (When you lift the beaters, the mixture will flow back onto the surface like a ribbon.) Add bourbon to chocolate mixture, then fold yolk-sugar mixture into chocolate mixture. Mix flour with pecans and fold into chocolate mixture. Using an electric mixer, whip egg whites and remaining half of sugar to form soft peaks, then fold into chocolate mixture. Pour batter into prepared pan and bake for 20 to 25 minutes (cake should test done with a toothpick but not dry). Allow cake to cool in pan and then place in the freezer for at least 2 hours. Once it's frozen, remove sides of springform pan. Invert cake onto a wire rack and remove bottom of springform pan.

Prepare ganache by bringing cream to a boil and pouring over chocolate chips in a bowl. Whisk until completely smooth. Set wire rack containing cake onto a sheet pan with sides. Pour lukewarm ganache over cake, coating completely, and repouring if necessary to cover well. Gently jiggle wire rack to help drain excess ganache. Ganache will lose its shine when set. Remove cake from wire rack with a wide spatula and place on a serving plate.

SERVES 10 TO 12

Chocolate Fudge Ribbon Cake

CAKE

1 18.25-ounce box fudge cake mix

1 3.9-ounce box instant chocolate
    pudding

½ cup milk

4 eggs

1 cup vegetable oil

1 teaspoon pure vanilla extract

1 cup chopped walnuts or pecans

FILLING

2 tablespoons butter, softened

1 tablespoon cornstarch

1 14-ounce can sweetened condensed
    milk

1 egg

1 teaspoon pure vanilla or almond
    extract

GLAZE

2 1-ounce squares semisweet
    chocolate

2 tablespoons butter

2 tablespoons water

2 tablespoons milk

1 cup confectioners' sugar, sifted

½ teaspoon pure vanilla or
    almond extract

Preheat oven to 325°F. Grease and flour a 10-inch Bundt pan.

Mix together cake mix, chocolate pudding, milk, eggs, oil, and vanilla in a large bowl. Beat for approximately 2 minutes, using an electric mixer, then stir in nuts. Pour half of batter into prepared pan. In separate bowl, beat butter and cornstarch together. Slowly add condensed milk. Add egg and vanilla and beat until smooth. Pour mixture evenly into Bundt pan containing half of batter. Pour other half on top. Bake for 1 hour or until done. Cool in pan for 10 minutes. Invert onto cake plate and allow to cool completely. While it cools, prepare glaze. In a small saucepan over medium-low heat, melt together chocolate, butter, and water. Stir until melted. Add milk and mix well. Remove from heat. Stir in sugar and vanilla, and continue stirring until smooth. Drizzle over cooled cake.

SERVES 16

Cool and Creamy Coconut Cake

THIS IS ONE OF THOSE easy, easy recipes that I think you'll just love and probably turn to time and time again.

1 18.25-ounce box yellow cake mix (plus ingredients to prepare)	1 8-ounce container frozen whipped topping, thawed
1 14-ounce can sweetened condensed milk	2½ to 3 cups flaked, sweetened coconut
1 15-ounce can cream of coconut	

Preheat oven to 350°F. Grease a 13 × 9 × 2-inch pan.

Prepare cake as directed on package. Pour batter into prepared pan and bake for time indicated on package. Remove cake from oven and, using a fork or skewer, poke holes in entire cake. Mix together condensed milk and cream of coconut and pour over warm cake. Cool cake completely. Frost with whipped topping and sprinkle top with coconut. Cover and refrigerate until ready to serve. This cake is best prepared a day or two before serving. Cut into squares to serve.

SERVES 20

Is It Really
Better Than Sex? Cake

IN MY FIRST COOKBOOK, The Lady & Sons Savannah Country Cookbook, *my Aunt Beth Hiers down in Winter Haven, Florida, shared with me one of her favorite cake recipes, Better Than Sex, Yes! Well, in today's mail I found a copy of a similar recipe, once again from my Aunt Beth: Is It Really Better Than Sex? Cake. What's up with you and all these sex cakes, girl?*

1 18.25-ounce box yellow cake mix (plus ingredients to prepare)	1 3.4-ounce box French vanilla pudding (plus ingredients to prepare)
1 20-ounce can crushed pineapple	1½ cups heavy cream
1⅓ cups sugar	1 cup flaked, sweetened coconut, toasted (see note)

Preheat oven to 350°F. Grease a 13 × 9 × 2-inch pan.

Prepare cake as directed on package. Pour into prepared pan. Bake 30 to 35 minutes. While cake is baking, combine pineapple and 1 cup of the sugar in a saucepan. Bring to a boil over medium heat, stirring constantly. Remove from heat and allow to cool slightly. Remove cake from oven and pierce holes in cake with a fork. Pour pineapple mixture over hot cake. Prepare pudding according to package directions. Spread over cake and refrigerate until thoroughly chilled. Before serving, beat cream and remaining sugar together with an electric mixer until stiff. Cover top of cake with whipped cream and sprinkle with toasted coconut.

To toast coconut, spread in a thin layer on a cookie sheet. Place in a 350°F oven. Watch very carefully because it can burn quickly. Stir as often as needed to ensure it browns evenly.

SERVES 16 TO 20

Chocolate Sybil Cake

311 WEST CONGRESS STREET, home of The Lady & Sons, is owned by Mr. and Mrs. Herman Barnett. A strong, charming, turn-of-the-century building, it originally was the home for Sears, Roebuck. When the Barnetts purchased the building in the 1950s it housed a shoe store before they started Barnett's Educational Supply House, which thrived for over forty years. Now it's home to The Lady & Sons. We have now occupied the building for six years, and we're pulling for thirty-four more, just like the Barnetts. I felt it only fitting to include a recipe from Mrs. Sybil Barnett's files.

CAKE	FROSTING
½ cup (1 stick) butter, softened	½ cup (1 stick) butter
1 cup sugar	½ cup semisweet chocolate chips
4 eggs	1 cup sugar
1 cup all-purpose flour	⅓ cup evaporated milk
1 teaspoon baking powder	1 teaspoon pure vanilla extract
⅛ teaspoon salt	½ cup chopped pecans or walnuts
1 teaspoon pure vanilla extract	
1 16-ounce can Hershey's chocolate syrup	

Preheat oven to 350°F. Grease and flour a 13 × 9 × 2-inch pan.

Using an electric mixer, cream butter and sugar together until light and fluffy. Add eggs one at a time, beating well after each addition. Sift flour, baking powder, and salt together in another bowl. Add to creamed mixture, continuing to beat. Add vanilla and chocolate syrup to batter and mix well. Pour into prepared pan and bake for 25 to 30 minutes. Just before cake is done, prepare frosting. Put butter, chocolate chips, sugar, and evaporated milk in a saucepan over medium heat and bring to a boil. Stirring ingredients together, boil for 2 to 3 minutes. Remove from heat and stir in vanilla and nuts. Pour over warm cake. Delicious!

SERVES 16 TO 20

Butter Pecan Cheesecake

NUTTY AND DELICIOUS.

CRUST

5 tablespoons butter, melted

1½ cups graham cracker crumbs

⅓ cup sugar

½ cup chopped pecans

FILLING

3 8-ounce packages cream cheese,
    at room temperature

1½ cups sugar

3 eggs

2 cups sour cream

1 teaspoon pure vanilla extract

1 teaspoon pure butter flavoring

½ teaspoon pure almond extract

1 cup chopped pecans

SAUCE

½ cup chopped pecans, toasted

1 cup Smucker's Special Recipe
    Butterscotch Caramel Ice
    Cream Topping

Whipped cream, for garnish

Preheat oven to 475°F.

For crust, pour butter over graham cracker crumbs, sugar, and pecans; stir well. Press into the bottom of a 9-inch springform pan. Set aside.

For filling, using an electric mixer, cream together cream cheese and sugar, beating well. Add eggs one at a time, beating well after each addition. Add sour cream, flavorings, and pecans and stir. Pour over crust and bake at 475°F for 10 minutes, then lower temperature to 300°F and bake for an additional 50 minutes. Turn off oven, open oven door, and let cake remain in oven for 1 hour. Remove from oven and allow to cool to room temperature. Cover and refrigerate. When ready to serve, remove ring from springform pan. Stir toasted pecans into butterscotch topping. Drizzle cake with topping mixture. Top each slice with a dollop of fresh whipped cream.

SERVES 12

Carolyn's Jell-O Cheesecake

THIS IS LOW IN CALORIES and real good! You may use any flavor of Jell-O and coordinate it with any fruit. You can also make this with sugar-added Jell-O.

1 12-ounce container low-fat (1%) cottage cheese	1 pint fresh strawberries, plus extra for garnish
3 0.3-ounce boxes sugar-free strawberry Jell-O	1 8-ounce container frozen lite whipped topping, thawed
2 ready-made lite graham cracker crusts	

Put cottage cheese in a blender. Make 2 boxes of the Jell-O, using 1 cup of hot, and 1 cup of cold water. At once, before it jells, add to cottage cheese. Blend until smooth. Pour into crust and refrigerate until set. Cut up fruit and place on top of pie. Make up remaining package Jell-O per instructions on box. Pour it on top of fruit and put it in refrigerator until set. Put whipped topping on top. Garnish with more fruit.

SERVES 12

Earthquake Cake

THIS TASTY CAKE will surely look like it registered a 9 on the Richter scale.

1 cup flaked, sweetened coconut	¼ cup (½ stick) butter, melted
1 cup chopped pecans	1 16-ounce box confectioners' sugar
1 18.25-ounce box German chocolate cake mix (plus ingredients to prepare)	1 8-ounce package cream cheese
	½ teaspoon pure almond extract

Preheat oven to 350°F. Grease and flour a 13 × 9 × 2-inch pan.

Spread coconut and pecans on bottom of pan. Mix cake according to package directions and pour over coconut and pecans. Mix sugar, butter, and cream cheese; spread over cake. Bake for 45 to 50 minutes.

SERVES 16 TO 20

Eclair Cake

CAKE	FROSTING
1 1-pound box graham crackers	1½ cups confectioners' sugar
2 3.4-ounce boxes instant French vanilla pudding	½ cup cocoa
3½ cups milk	3 tablespoons butter, softened
1 8-ounce container frozen whipped topping, thawed	3 tablespoons milk
	2 teaspoons light corn syrup
	2 teaspoons pure vanilla extract

Butter the bottom of a 13 × 9 × 2-inch pan. Line with whole graham crackers. In bowl of an electric mixer, mix pudding with milk; beat at medium speed for 2 minutes. Fold in whipped topping. Pour half the pudding mixture over graham crackers. Place another layer of whole graham crackers on top of pudding layer. Pour over remaining half of pudding mixture and cover with another layer of graham crackers.

For frosting, blend together sugar and cocoa. Add butter and milk, mixing well. Add corn syrup and vanilla. Stir until creamy. Cover cake with frosting and refrigerate for 24 hours.

SERVES 20 TO 24

Fresh Pear Cake

2 cups sugar	1 teaspoon allspice
3 cups all-purpose flour	1½ cups vegetable oil
1½ teaspoons baking soda	3 eggs
1½ teaspoons salt	1 teaspoon pure vanilla extract
1 teaspoon cinnamon	3 cups peeled, cored, diced pears
1 teaspoon cloves	(about 5 pears)

Preheat oven to 350°F. Grease and flour a 10-inch Bundt pan.

Sift sugar, flour, baking soda, salt, cinnamon, cloves, and allspice together into a large bowl. Add oil, eggs, vanilla, and pears; mix well. Pour mixture into prepared pan and bake for 1¼ hours or until done.

SERVES 20 TO 24

Icebox Fruitcake

FOLKS, THIS RECIPE is so unbelievable. I am not a big fruitcake fan. However, I do enjoy my Icebox Fruitcake. Not only is this so very good, it's easy to make.

These are good to give as gifts at Christmas time. Use mini-loaf pans.

1 14-ounce can sweetened condensed milk	1 3.5-ounce can flaked, sweetened coconut
1 16-ounce bag miniature marshmallows	2 8-ounce packages chopped dates
1-pound box graham crackers, crushed	1 16-ounce jar maraschino cherry halves, well-drained
4 cups pecans	½ cup bourbon

Grease a 9 × 5 × 3-inch loaf pan.

Heat milk and marshmallows together over low heat. Stir until marshmallows are melted (stir constantly because condensed milk scorches easily!). Remove from heat. Combine graham crackers, pecans, coconut, dates, and cherries in a bowl. Add bourbon to milk-marshmallow mixture and pour over graham cracker mixture. Mix well (I've found my hands work well for this procedure). Scoop mixture into prepared pan and mold to fit the pan. Pack the mixture tightly so there are no air pockets. Refrigerate for 2 days or longer before serving.

Cut ½-inch slices to serve.

Line your loaf pan with parchment paper for easier removal of the cake. Simply cut the parchment paper to cover the bottom and sides of the pan and overlap the paper outside the pan so you can lift the cake out after refrigeration.

YIELDS ABOUT 15 SLICES

Italian Crème Cake

CAKE

1 cup (2 sticks) butter, softened

2 cups granulated sugar

5 eggs

2 cups all-purpose flour

1 teaspoon baking soda

1 cup buttermilk

2 teaspoons pure vanilla extract

1 3.5-ounce can angel flaked, sweetened coconut

1 cup nuts, chopped

FROSTING

1 8-ounce package cream cheese, softened

¼ cup (½ stick) butter, softened

1 16-ounce box confectioners' sugar

1 teaspoon pure almond extract

Preheat oven to 350°F. Grease and flour three 9-inch cake pans.

Using an electric mixer, cream together butter and granulated sugar. Add eggs one at a time, beating well after each addition. Stir together the flour and baking soda. Add alternately with buttermilk to sugar mixture, being sure to begin and end with flour. Stir in vanilla, coconut, and nuts. Pour into prepared pans. Bake for about 30 minutes, checking cakes after 20 minutes. Allow to cool 5 minutes in pans. Invert onto rack and cool completely.

Meanwhile, to prepare frosting, cream together cream cheese and butter. Add confectioners' sugar and almond. Beat until smooth. Stack cakes into 3 layers; spread frosting between layers.

SERVES 16 TO 20

Grandma Paul's Japanese Fruitcake

WHEN I WAS a child, Christmas didn't come to our house or Grandmother Paul's house without one of these big beautiful cakes on the counter. I sometimes frost this cake at the last minute with a 7-Minute Icing (see page 22).

CAKE

1 cup vegetable shortening

2 cups sugar

4 eggs

3 cups sifted all-purpose flour

2 teaspoons baking powder

1 teaspoon salt

1 cup milk

1 teaspoon pure vanilla extract

SPICE LAYER

1 teaspoon cinnamon

½ teaspoon cloves

1 teaspoon allspice

½ cup raisins, dusted with a little flour

½ cup nuts

FILLING AND TOPPING

2 cups sugar

2 tablespoons cornstarch

1 cup boiling water

1 20-ounce can crushed pineapple, drained

1 cup grated coconut

Juice and zest of 2 lemons

½ cup maraschino cherry halves

Preheat oven to 350°F. Grease and flour three 9-inch cake pans.

Using an electric mixer, cream together shortening and sugar until fluffy. Add eggs one at a time, beating well after each addition. Stir together flour, baking powder, and salt in another bowl. Add flour mixture alternately with milk to creamed mixture, beginning and ending with flour. Add vanilla and mix well. Divide batter into thirds. Pour one third into each of 2 prepared pans. To remaining one third of batter, add spice layer ingredients, folding in well. Pour into remaining prepared pan. Bake for 25 to 30 minutes.

To prepare filling and topping, stir together sugar and cornstarch in a saucepan. Add water, pineapple, coconut, and lemon juice and zest. Stir together and cook over medium heat until thick enough to spread onto cake layers. Remove from heat, stir in cherries, and allow to cool slightly. When stacking, place spice layer in the middle. Spread filling on layers, sides, and top.

SERVES 16 TO 20

Orange-Walnut Sunrise Coffee Cake

<PERFECTLY WONDERFUL> *and perfectly easy.*

1 17.3-ounce can Pillsbury Grands! refrigerated flaky biscuits	½ cup confectioners' sugar
¼ cup finely chopped walnuts	1½ ounces (½ a 3-ounce bar) cream cheese, softened
⅓ cup granulated sugar	1 tablespoon orange juice, or more as necessary
2 teaspoons grated orange peel	
2 tablespoons butter, melted	

Preheat oven to 375°F. Grease a 9-inch round cake pan.

Separate biscuit dough into 8 biscuits. Place 1 biscuit in center of pan. Cut remaining biscuits in half, forming 14 half circles. Arrange pieces around center biscuit with cut sides facing same direction. In a small bowl, combine walnuts, granulated sugar, and orange peel and mix well. Brush butter over tops of biscuits and sprinkle with walnut mixture. Bake for 20 minutes or until golden brown.

Meanwhile, in a small bowl, combine confectioners' sugar, cream cheese, and enough orange juice for desired drizzling consistency. Blend until smooth, then drizzle over warm coffee cake. Cool 10 minutes. Serve warm.

SERVES 8

Granite Steps Country Blueberry Coffee Cake

THIS DELICIOUS COFFEE CAKE *is sometimes served at breakfast time to the guests at the Granite Steps Bed and Breakfast here in Savannah.*

½ cup packed light brown sugar

½ teaspoon cinnamon

1 12-ounce can Pillsbury Big Country buttermilk biscuits

½ cup (1 stick) butter, melted, plus 2 tablespoons, cut into small pieces

1 cup quick-cooking rolled oats

1½ cups fresh or frozen blueberries

¼ cup granulated sugar

Preheat oven to 375°F. Generously grease a 9-inch square baking dish.

In a small bowl, combine brown sugar and cinnamon and mix well with a fork. Separate biscuit dough into 10 biscuits. Cut each biscuit into quarters, and dip each piece in melted butter and coat with brown sugar mixture. Arrange in a single layer in baking dish. Sprinkle with ½ cup of the oats. Combine blueberries and granulated sugar in a bowl and toss to coat. Spoon over oats and biscuits and sprinkle with remaining ½ cup oats. Top with butter pieces. Bake for 30 to 35 minutes or until cake is golden brown and center is done. Cool for 20 minutes. Serve warm.

SERVES 8

Key Lime
Mousse Cake

I RECENTLY RECONNECTED *with a cousin whom I was very close to as a child; we had not spoken in more than thirty years! The really sad part is that she resides in Atlanta, Georgia, not Tokyo, Japan. She called to invite me to the celebration of the matriarch's (on my mother's side of the family) ninetieth birthday. All of a sudden I was very anxious to see my cousin Johnnie Gabriel after all these years.*

We had such a wonderful time at the party, giggling and recounting stories from our childhood. Johnnie said she'd never forget the summer that I traumatized her by delivering news that changed her life: "There's no Santa Claus, Johnnie." Now bear in mind that Johnnie was two years older than me; this girl was really leading a sheltered life!

One summer night Johnnie sat me in the middle of her bed after the grown-ups were safely asleep. She handed me a single-edged razor blade (no handle), and told me to shave my legs. I very painstakingly spent two hours shaving my dry legs with that razor. Girls, do I have to tell you how bad my legs hurt the next day? I guess this was payback for the devastating news I had delivered to her a few summers earlier.

Johnnie, like so many other members of the Paul family, had a passion for food and food preparation. She had opened Gabriel's Desserts, a fabulous bakery in Marietta, a suburb of Atlanta. Like mine, her business was born out of necessity and began in the tiny confines of her home kitchen with limited resources. We were both fortunate to get beyond the major obstacles that occur when entrepreneurs begin their dream.

I told Johnnie that I was in the middle of writing my next cookbook, The Lady & Sons Just Desserts, *and said how thrilled I would be if she would share a recipe or two with me.*

Not only did she share this recipe, which happens to be her husband's favorite, she also has shared her Chocolate Bourbon Pecan Cake (page 30) and her White Chocolate Macadamia Nut Pie (page 78).

I made a vow at that moment to keep alive the friendship that began so many years ago.

CRUST

2 cups crushed graham crackers

¼ cup sugar

½ cup (1 stick) butter, melted

FILLING

6 tablespoons fresh Key lime juice
(use bottled if fresh limes are
unavailable)

1 ¼-ounce package (1 envelope)
unflavored gelatin

2½ cups heavy cream

10 1-ounce squares Baker's
premium white chocolate,
chopped, plus 1 to 1½ ounces,
grated or shaved into curls

3 8-ounce packages cream cheese,
softened

1 cup sugar

1½ tablespoons lime zest

For crust, mix together cracker crumbs, sugar, and butter. Press into the bottom of a 10-inch springform pan and 1 inch up the sides. Set aside.

For filling, squeeze or pour lime juice into a bowl and sprinkle gelatin in to soften. Bring ½ cup of the heavy cream to a simmer in a saucepan, remove from heat, and add the 10 ounces white chocolate, stirring until smooth. Stir in gelatin and lime juice and allow to cool. Using an electric mixer, blend together cream cheese, sugar, and lime zest. Slowly beat cooled white chocolate mixture into cream cheese mixture. Using clean, dry beaters, beat remaining 2 cups heavy cream until it peaks. Fold into white chocolate mixture, then pour into pie crust. Cover and freeze overnight. Remove from freezer and run a sharp knife around inside of springform pan to help loosen cake. Release springform ring from pan, move cake to a serving plate, and grate or curl the 1 to 1½ ounces white chocolate over cake. Cut into wedges with a knife that has been dipped into hot water.

SERVES 14 TO 16

Ludovic's Mom's Chocolate Cake

SOUTHERN GIRL VERSUS *a French chef—the only thing we had in common was that we both started at our grandmothers' sides. It was our debut on the Food Network's "Ready . . . Set . . . Cook!" a television cooking game show that pits two chefs against each other before a live studio audience.*

Can you imagine my fright when I learned I was going up against Ludovic Lefebvre, one of the top French chefs in America, executive chef of L'Orangerie in Los Angeles, California? I'm the Georgia girl who's a graduate of the School of Hard Knocks, magna cum laude. I've tried to think of some other way to describe my terror. But I can't think of nothing else; just know I was scared to death.

Even though there was a world of difference between the two of us, we went on to do four great shows together, having more fun than a barrel of monkeys. I'll never forget the show in which we were given canned refrigerated biscuits to prepare—I looked over and saw Ludovic steady-opening the can with a can opener and watched the biscuits explode in his face!

The cooking gods must have been shining on me that day, or maybe they were taking a nap. Because somehow I managed to win three out of four competitions. We'll take it any way we can get it, won't we, girls?

Ludovic has been kind enough to share with us his loving mother's best chocolate cake recipe. This chocolate cake is also a favorite on the menu at L'Orangerie. Thank you, Ludovic, for you will always remain a special part of a very special day.

CAKE	4 eggs
1 cup bittersweet chocolate, melted	5 tablespoons all-purpose flour
1 cup (2 sticks) butter, melted	GRANITÉ
1 cup sugar	1 quart milk
½ cup water	7 tablespoons sugar

Preheat oven to 350°F. Generously grease an 8-inch springform pan.

Combine chocolate and butter in a bowl. Bring sugar and water to a boil in a saucepan. Remove from heat and add chocolate mixture. Mix together eggs and flour, then add to chocolate mixture. Pour into prepared pan. Set springform pan in a larger pan containing warm water (in French, this is referred to as a *bain-marie*; in English, this simply means a water bath). The water should reach about an inch up sides of springform pan. Bake for an hour, or until done (cake will be somewhat custard-like). Remove this delicate cake from oven and cool completely before removing the ring of the springform pan and transferring cake to a plate.

To prepare the granité, boil the milk and sugar together, about a minute. Remove from heat. Pour into a baking pan and place in freezer. Using a fork, scrape the granité every half hour as it ices up. It is ready when the mixture resembles slush. Serve on the side of the cake.

SERVES 8

Mystery Mocha Cake

A CHOCOHOLIC'S DELIGHT! Serve with ice cream for a special treat.

¾ cup granulated sugar, plus ½ cup	½ cup milk
1 cup all-purpose flour	1 teaspoon pure vanilla extract
2 teaspoons baking powder	4 tablespoons cocoa
1 1-ounce square semisweet chocolate	½ cup packed light brown sugar
2 tablespoons butter	1 cup coffee (liquid)

Preheat oven to 350°F. Grease a 9-inch square pan. Mix together the ¾ cup granulated sugar, flour, and baking powder.

Melt together chocolate and butter in a saucepan and add to flour mixture. Add milk and vanilla, mixing well. Pour mixture into prepared pan. Combine the ½ cup granulated sugar, cocoa, and brown sugar. Sprinkle over batter. Pour coffee on top of this and do not stir. Bake for 30 to 35 minutes. (Cake should have a chocolate syrup base on the bottom.) Cut cake into 9 serving pieces. Invert onto serving plate and spoon extra cocoa mixture over cake if desired. This cake is best when served warm.

SERVES 9

Old South
Jelly Roll Cake

4 eggs, separated

¾ cup granulated sugar

1 tablespoon pure vanilla extract

¾ cup sifted cake flour

¾ teaspoon baking powder

¼ teaspoon salt

Confectioner's sugar, sifted, for dusting, plus some for sprinkling

1 cup jam or jelly, stirred well

Whipped cream, for garnish

Preheat oven to 400°F. Line a 15 × 10 × 1-inch jelly roll pan with waxed paper.

In a small bowl, beat egg whites until stiff but not dry; set aside. In another bowl, beat egg yolks until light; gradually add granulated sugar and vanilla. Sift together flour, baking powder, and salt; add to egg yolk mixture. Fold in egg whites and pour batter into prepared pan. Bake for 8 to 10 minutes or until light brown. Loosen edges of cake, then invert cake onto a lint-free towel dusted with confectioners' sugar (this will prevent the cake from sticking to the towel).

Gently peel waxed paper from cake. Trim ¼-inch hard crust off each long side of the jelly roll cake (this will allow you to roll the cake without it splitting). Beginning with the narrow side, roll cake and towel up together. Cool cake on rack, seam side down, for 10 to 15 minutes. Gently unroll and spread cake with jam or jelly and re-roll. Sprinkle with confectioners' sugar or spread with whipped cream.

SERVES 8 TO 10

Plum Cake

CAKE	2 4-ounce jars strained plum
1 cup vegetable oil	baby food with tapioca
2 cups granulated sugar	1 cup chopped pecans
3 eggs	GLAZE
1 teaspoon ground cloves	1 cup confectioners' sugar
1 teaspoon ground cinnamon	Juice of 1 lemon
2 cups self-rising flour	

Preheat oven to 350°F. Grease and flour a 10-inch Bundt pan.

Mix oil, granulated sugar, eggs, cloves, cinnamon, flour, and plum baby food in large bowl of an electric mixer. Beat at a medium speed for 3 to 4 minutes. Stir in pecans. Pour into prepared pan. Bake 1 hour and 10 minutes. Remove from oven and allow to cool for 10 minutes. Meanwhile, to prepare glaze, mix confectioners' sugar and lemon juice together until smooth. Invert cake onto plate. With a large fork, pierce holes in top of cake and pour glaze over while still warm.

SERVES 16 TO 18

Savannah Date Nut Cake

1 8-ounce box chopped dates	3 eggs
1 teaspoon baking soda	3 tablespoons orange marmalade
1 cup boiling water	1½ cups chopped pecans, ½ cup reserved for topping
3 cups all-purpose flour	
1 cup raisins, chopped	1 teaspoon pure vanilla extract
¼ teaspoon salt	1 6-ounce jar maraschino cherry halves
1 cup (2 sticks) butter, softened	
2 cups packed light brown sugar	

Preheat oven to 325°F. Grease and flour a 10-inch Bundt pan.

Put dates and baking soda into boiling water in a saucepan, then turn off heat and set aside.

Combine flour, raisins, and salt. Using an electric mixer, cream together butter and sugar; add eggs, marmalade, 1 cup of the chopped nuts, vanilla, and date mixture. Add flour mixture ½ cup at a time, beating well. Pour batter into prepared pan. Bake 1½ hours. Just as cake begins to brown, without removing cake from oven, sprinkle with remaining ½ cup nuts and cherry halves. Close oven door and continue to bake for remaining time. Cool in pan for 10 minutes, then invert onto a cake plate to continue cooling.

SERVES 16 TO 20

Southwest Georgia Pound Cake

I WOULD LIKE TO SAY a few things about the woman this book is dedicated to—my sweet mother. That beautiful, kind, genteel, and gracious red-haired lady will always remain young in my heart and mind, for she left this earth at the age of forty-four after succumbing to cancer. Her untimely death was devastating, and I had to remind myself more than once that although the quantity of time was not there, the quality couldn't have been better.

I remember preparing supper for her and my husband as a nineteen-year-old bride. At the end of the meal she looked at me and said, "Honey, you're gonna be a better cook than your mother."

I was dumbstruck. I blurted out, "No way, Mama."

Nobody could cook better than my mama, but I remember my mama thinking the same way about my grandmother's cooking. I remember my daddy saying, "Red, you're a better cook than your mother." I don't think Mama ever quite believed this, just as I didn't believe it when she said that about me.

Mama had several different pound cake recipes, but I think this was probably one of our favorites. This cake is great topped with fresh strawberries and vanilla ice cream, and (if you want it to be really good) topped with a dollop of fresh sweetened whipped cream. I promise you won't find a better strawberry shortcake anywhere. This is also wonderful sliced, buttered, and toasted for breakfast along with a dollop of preserves, jelly, or jam. And don't forget a cup of good hot coffee.

1 cup (2 sticks) butter, softened	½ teaspoon salt
3 cups sugar	1 cup heavy cream
6 eggs	2 teaspoons pure vanilla extract (you may use lemon or almond flavoring instead)
3 cups all-purpose flour	
½ teaspoon baking powder	

Generously grease and flour a 10-inch Bundt pan.

Using an electric mixer, cream butter and sugar together until fluffy. Add eggs one at a time, beating well after each addition. Sift together flour, baking powder, and salt. Alternately add flour mixture and heavy cream to butter-sugar mixture, beginning and ending with flour. Stir in flavoring. Pour batter into prepared pan. Place in a cold oven, set oven temperature at 325°F, and bake for 1¼ hours without opening oven door. Bake for an additional 15 minutes if necessary. Remove from oven and cool in pan for 15 minutes. Invert cake onto cake plate, and for a real treat, serve yourself a slice while it's still warm.

SERVES 16 TO 20

Bobby's Caramel Cake (pg 23)

Key Lime Grits Pie (pg 71)

Icebox Fruitcake (pg 38)

Fruit Slush (pg 147), Mother's Nut Rolls (pg 149)

Cassata Cake (pg 105)

Banana Split Brownie Pizza (pg 137)

Pineapple Gooey Butter Cake (pg 82)

TOP RIGHT: Chocolate Cheese Fudge (pg 121), Pine Bark (pg 128),
Uncle Bubba's Benne Candy (pg 132), Microwave Peanut Brittle (pg 129)

Sweet Baby Carrot Cake

What would I do without my mortgage banker and friend, Jackie Mullins? When I need mortgage money and she throws it my way, I can always expect to find a few good recipes thrown in as well. This is one of 'em. What a banker!

Notice that this recipe does not call for nuts. You may add chopped nuts to the batter or frosting, or you may simply sprinkle the frosted cake with chopped nuts. Regardless, just make sure you try this cake because it is truly the easiest of all carrot cake recipes.

CAKE	FROSTING
2 cups self-rising flour	¼ cup (½ stick) butter, softened
2 teaspoons ground cinnamon	1 8-ounce package cream cheese, softened
2 4-ounce jars strained carrot baby food	1 16-ounce box confectioners' sugar
4 eggs	1 teaspoon pure vanilla extract
2 cups granulated sugar	
1½ cups vegetable oil	

Preheat oven to 325°F. Grease and flour three 8- or 9-inch cake pans.

Mix all cake ingredients together and blend well with a handheld electric mixer. Pour batter into prepared pans. Bake for 25 to 30 minutes, or until golden brown. Allow to cool in pan for 5 minutes. Invert onto lint-free dishcloth, or waxed paper, and allow to cool completely. For frosting, mix all ingredients with handheld electric mixer and blend until smooth and creamy. Frost layers, top, and sides of cooled cake.

SERVES 16

Tennessee Banana–Black Walnut Cake with Caramel Frosting

Do NOT SUBSTITUTE English walnuts for black walnuts.

CAKE	FROSTING
½ cup vegetable shortening	½ cup (1 stick) butter, softened
1½ cups granulated sugar	1 cup packed dark brown sugar
2 eggs	⅓ cup heavy cream, plus more as necessary
1 cup mashed bananas	
4 tablespoons buttermilk	1 tablespoon pure vanilla extract
1 teaspoon pure vanilla extract	1 16-ounce box confectioners' sugar
2 cups all-purpose flour	
½ teaspoon baking soda	
1 cup chopped black walnuts	

Preheat oven to 350°F. Grease and flour two 9-inch cake pans.

Using an electric mixer, cream together shortening and granulated sugar in a bowl. Add eggs one at a time and mix well after each addition. Stir in mashed bananas, buttermilk, and vanilla. Mix flour and baking soda and add. Mix in black walnuts. Pour into prepared pans. Bake for 35 minutes. Cool in pans for 10 minutes. Remove from pans and cool completely.

Meanwhile, prepare frosting. Melt butter in saucepan. Add brown sugar and cream. Cook over medium-low heat for about 2 minutes, until the sugar is dissolved. Remove from heat and add vanilla. Using a handheld electric mixer, beat in confectioners' sugar until smooth. If frosting is too thick, add 1 tablespoon heavy cream at a time until consistency is right.

SERVES 12

The Bag Lady's Favorite Chocolate Pound Cake

IN THE EARLY DAYS of *The Bag Lady*, this cake was definitely one of those foods on the top of my customers' love list. I made sure that I baked and served it at least once a week. I hope you love it too.

This cake freezes very well and is a great treat to have on hand for unexpected or drop-in company.

Die-hard chocoholics might want to just throw on their favorite chocolate icing.

3 cups all-purpose flour	½ cup vegetable shortening
½ teaspoon baking soda	3 cups sugar
½ teaspoon baking powder	5 eggs
½ teaspoon salt	1 cup buttermilk
5 tablespoons cocoa	1 tablespoon pure vanilla extract
1 cup (2 sticks) butter, softened	

Preheat oven to 325°F. Grease and flour a 10-inch Bundt pan.

Sift together flour, baking soda, baking powder, salt, and cocoa and set aside. Using an electric mixer, cream together butter, shortening, and sugar until fluffy. Add eggs one at a time and mix well after each addition. Add flour and buttermilk alternately to butter mixture, beginning and ending with flour. Add vanilla and mix well. Pour batter into prepared pan. Bake for 1¾ hours, or until cake is done. Remove from oven and allow cake to cool in pan for 10 minutes. Invert onto cake plate and serve.

SERVES 16

Turtle Cake

CAKE	FROSTING
1 18.25-ounce box German chocolate cake mix (plus ingredients to prepare)	3 tablespoons cocoa
	¼ cup (½ stick) butter
	⅓ cup milk
1 14-ounce package caramel candies	1 tablespoon light corn syrup
½ cup (1 stick) butter	⅛ teaspoon salt
1 14-ounce can sweetened condensed milk	2 cups confectioners' sugar
1 6-ounce package semisweet chocolate chips	1 teaspoon pure vanilla extract
1 cup chopped nuts	

Preheat oven to 350°F. Grease a 13 × 9 × 2-inch pan.

Prepare cake according to directions on box. Pour half of batter into prepared pan. Reserve other half. Bake for 15 minutes. Remove from oven and cool completely. (Don't turn off oven.) Meanwhile, melt caramel candies with butter in a saucepan. When completely melted, remove from heat and stir in condensed milk until smooth. Let mixture cool completely. Add chocolate chips and nuts. Spread mixture over cooled cake. Pour remaining batter over mixture and return to oven for another 25 to 30 minutes.

While cake is baking, prepare frosting. Mix together cocoa, butter, milk, corn syrup, and salt in a saucepan over medium heat. Bring ingredients to a full rolling boil and allow to boil for approximately 3 minutes, stirring occasionally. Remove from heat. Using a handheld electric mixer, beat confectioners' sugar and vanilla into cocoa mixture; beat until smooth. Pour icing over warm cake.

SERVES 16 TO 20

Wilkes-Barre
Cream Cheese Cake

CRUST

½ cup (1 stick) butter, softened

½ cup sugar

2 eggs

1½ cups all-purpose flour

1 teaspoon baking powder

FILLING

2 8-ounce packages cream cheese,
    softened

1 cup sugar

4 egg yolks, beaten, whites
    reserved

Pinch of salt

1 teaspoon pure vanilla extract

3 cups milk, at room
    temperature

Cinnamon, for sprinkling

Preheat oven to 350°F. Lightly grease a 15 × 10 × 1-inch jelly roll pan.

Blend all crust ingredients well with a handheld electric mixer. Pat into prepared pan. Cover bottom and sides of pan. Dampen fingertips with water for easier patting.

Combine all filling ingredients in a bowl except egg whites, salt, and cinnamon; blend with a handheld electric mixer until smooth. In another bowl, beat egg whites, with salt, until stiff. Fold into cream cheese mixture. (This filling will be on the thin side.)

Pour over crust and sprinkle with cinnamon. Bake for 50 to 60 minutes, or until filling is set. Cool completely before serving.

SERVES 24

Wilmington Island Marsh Mud Cake

I AM FORTUNATE ENOUGH *to live on beautiful Wilmington Island, where my home sits directly on Turner's Creek. There's nothing more wonderful and peaceful than looking out my window and seeing the porpoises playing and gliding through the water, or the herons stalking the minnows in the tidewater creeks. Many homes on the island sit either on the water or the marsh—any way you look at it, we all see our share of mud here. Since this is one of the favorite cakes baked out here, I think that the name is very befitting.*

CAKE	FROSTING
½ cup cocoa	1 16-ounce box light brown sugar
1 cup (2 sticks) butter, melted	⅓ cup cocoa
4 eggs, beaten	¼ cup (½ stick) butter, softened
1½ cups all-purpose flour	½ cup milk
2 cups granulated sugar	1 teaspoon pure vanilla extract
⅛ teaspoon salt	1 10.5-ounce package miniature
1 teaspoon vanilla extract	marshmallows
1½ cups chopped pecans	

Preheat oven to 350°F. Grease a 13 × 9 × 2-inch pan.

Stir cocoa into mixing bowl with butter. Add eggs, flour, granulated sugar, salt, and vanilla. Beat well with a handheld electric mixer. Stir in nuts. Pour into prepared pan. Bake for 35 minutes. While cake is baking, prepare frosting. Mix brown sugar, cocoa, butter, milk, and vanilla together in a bowl and beat until smooth. Remove cake from oven and pour marshmallows over hot cake. Pour frosting over marshmallows on top.

SERVES 16 TO 20

Pies

Apple Butter Pumpkin Pie ❧ Chocolate Chip Pie ❧ Christmas Nut
Pie ❧ Coconut Pie ❧ Crunch Top Apple Pie ❧ Douglas's Dark
Rum Pecan Pie ❧ May Howard Elementary's Pie Winners: *Olivia's*
Buttermilk Pie ❧ *Laura's Peanut Butter Pie* ❧ *Lauren's Chocolate*
Drizzle Pie ❧ Frozen Peach Pie Filling ❧ Georgia Cracker Pie ❧
Green Tomato Pie ❧ Grits Pie ❧ Key Lime Grits Pie ❧ John
Berendt's Favorite Angel Pie ❧ Lemon Birdie Pie ❧ Lemon Chess
Pie ❧ Sean Jones Sweet Potato Pie ❧ Sin-sational Pie ❧ Snickers Pie
❧ White Chocolate Macadamia Nut Pie

1. When baking custard-type pies, brush the entire shell with a slightly beaten egg white. Pierce holes in the bottom of the crust with a fork. Run the crust under a hot broiler for a couple of minutes. (If you're concerned about the rim of the crust getting too dark, wrap a strip of aluminum foil around the edge.) This procedure will help in making the bottom of the pie not appear raw after pie is baked.

2. When making meringues for your pie, you will always require the use of an electric mixer.

3. Egg whites will produce a better meringue (and more of it!) if the eggs are at room temperature. Save the yolks for later use.

4. Avoid making meringues on a rainy day. The humidity in the air may cause failure.

5. When making pie crusts from scratch, handle and work the dough as little as possible. When rolling out the dough, dust the rolling pin and the work surface with half granulated sugar and half flour.

6. Frozen pie crusts come in aluminum pie plates. Refrigerated pie crusts come in a box, in the dairy section of your grocery store. These crusts are placed into your own pie plates.

Apple Butter Pumpkin Pie

THIS PIE RECIPE was given to me by June Royals Foster in loving memory of her mother, Virgie Royals. June says it's wonderful served slightly warm with sweetened fresh whipped cream.

1 cup apple butter	⅛ teaspoon ginger
1 cup fresh or canned pumpkin	3 eggs, slightly beaten
½ cup packed brown sugar	¾ cup evaporated milk
½ teaspoon salt	1 unbaked 9-inch pie shell
¾ teaspoon cinnamon	Sweetened whipped cream, for garnish (optional)
¾ teaspoon nutmeg	

Preheat oven to 425°F.

Combine apple butter, pumpkin, sugar, salt, and spices in a bowl. Stir in eggs. Gradually add milk and mix well. Pour into pie shell. Bake for about 40 minutes or until set.

SERVES 6

Chocolate Chip Pie

SERVE WITH VANILLA ICE CREAM or sweetened whipped cream.

1 cup sugar	1 cup pecans
½ cup all-purpose flour	1 cup semisweet chocolate chips
2 eggs, beaten	1 teaspoon pure vanilla extract
½ cup (1 stick) butter, melted and cooled	1 unbaked 9-inch pie shell

Preheat oven to 325°F.

Mix sugar and flour together in a bowl; add eggs, butter, pecans, chocolate chips, and vanilla, and stir. Pour into unbaked pie shell and bake for 45 to 60 minutes or until set.

SERVES 6 TO 8

Christmas Nut Pie

PERFECT FOR THE HARRIED holiday rush, and the Christmas Eve table.

½ cup (1 stick) butter, melted	½ cup flaked coconut
1 cup sugar	½ cup raisins
⅛ teaspoon salt	1 cup chopped walnuts
2 eggs, slightly beaten	1 teaspoon pure vanilla extract
1 tablespoon white vinegar	1 unbaked 9-inch pie shell

Preheat oven to 350°F.

Mix all ingredients together in a bowl until well blended. Pour into unbaked pie shell and bake for 40 to 50 minutes or until set.

SERVES 6 TO 8

Coconut Pie

THIS RECIPE IS SO VERY GOOD—it borders on the edge of tasting like an egg custard. And it has the Paula Deen bonus—it's easy!

½ cup (1 stick) butter	1 cup grated coconut
1½ cups sugar	1 teaspoon pure vanilla extract
5 eggs, beaten	2 unbaked 9-inch pie shells
¾ cup buttermilk	

Preheat oven to 350°F.

Melt butter, pour over sugar in a bowl, and blend. Add remaining ingredients and mix well. Pour equal amounts of mixture into pie shells. Bake for 45 to 50 minutes or until set and golden brown.

SERVES 12

Crunch Top Apple Pie

NOT YOUR TYPICAL apple pie.

CRUST AND FILLING

Dough for a double crust 9-inch pie (homemade, frozen, or refrigerated)

¾ cup sugar

1 tablespoon all-purpose flour

1 teaspoon ground cinnamon

Dash of salt

3½ cups peeled, chopped cooking apples

1 16-ounce jar applesauce

1 tablespoon lemon juice

2 tablespoons butter, chopped into small pieces

CRUNCH TOPPING

3 tablespoons all-purpose flour

1 tablespoon sugar

Dash of salt

1 tablespoon butter, at room temperature

Preheat oven to 425°F.

Line a 9-inch pie pan with half of dough. Combine sugar, flour, cinnamon, and salt in a bowl. Stir in apples, applesauce, and lemon juice. Spoon apple mixture into pie pan and dot with butter. Cut remaining crust into strips; arrange in a lattice design over top of pie.

For crunch topping, combine flour, sugar, and salt in a bowl. Using a fork, cut in butter until mixture is crumbly. Sprinkle over top of crust. Bake at 425°F for 10 minutes, then reduce heat to 350°F and continue to bake for about 45 minutes, or until crust and topping are golden brown.

SERVES 6 TO 8

Douglas's
Dark Rum Pecan Pie

I ALWAYS LOOK FORWARD to having my friend Douglas Boyce come to Savannah to celebrate Saint Patrick's Day with me and my family. Because we know Douglas is gonna be making and serving us up the meanest margaritas in town. And you know what? His pies ain't bad, either!

1 cup sugar	2 tablespoons Myers's Original Dark Rum (1 for the pie, 1 for you!)
3 tablespoons butter, melted	
½ cup dark Karo syrup	1 unbaked deep-dish 9-inch pie shell
3 large eggs, beaten	
1½ to 2 cups pecan halves, according to taste	

Preheat oven to 375°F.

Combine sugar and butter in a bowl; stir in syrup, eggs, pecans, and rum. Pour into unbaked pie shell; place on heavy-duty cookie sheet. Bake at 375°F for 10 minutes. Lower oven temperature to 350°F and continue to bake for an additional 25 minutes, or until pie is set. Remove from oven and allow to cool.

SERVES 6 TO 8

May Howard Elementary's Pie Winners

I WAS ASKED TO JUDGE a student pie-cooking contest at May Howard Elementary. With tongue in cheek, I said, "This'll be a piece a cake."

There were probably close to forty pies, and I felt obligated to taste every single solitary one. It was very hard to settle on the winners because the children had done an amazing job. The fact that I had overeaten and was feeling real sick to my stomach didn't help matters either. Eatin' forty pies is work! Fortunately, we were able to finally come up with a first, second, and third place winner.

- First Place—Olivia's Buttermilk Pie
  Olivia Rose Lanier, third grade, daughter of Mr. and Mrs. Allen Lanier

- Second Place—Laura's Peanut Butter Pie
  Laura Holland, fourth grade, daughter of Mr. and Mrs. Greg Holland

- Third Place—Lauren's Chocolate Drizzle Pie
  Lauren Burke, fifth grade, daughter of Mr. and Mrs. Ray Burke, Jr.

Olivia's Buttermilk Pie

SERVE WITH FRESH MIXED FRUIT or a dollop of fresh whipped cream, if desired (that's what Olivia says to do!).

1½ cups sugar	1 teaspoon pure vanilla extract
1 cup buttermilk	3 eggs
½ cup Bisquick	
⅓ cup (5⅓ tablespoons) butter, melted	

Preheat oven to 350°F. Grease a 9-inch pie pan.

Put all ingredients in a bowl and blend for 1 minute with a handheld electric mixer. Pour mixture into prepared pan. Bake for about 50 minutes or until a toothpick inserted in the center comes out clean. Cool for 5 minutes.

SERVES 6 TO 8

Laura's Peanut Butter Pie

CRUST	1 5.1-ounce box instant vanilla pudding
1½ cups all-purpose flour	
½ teaspoon salt	2½ cups milk
½ cup vegetable oil	1 8-ounce container frozen whipped topping, thawed
2 tablespoons granulated sugar	
2 teaspoons milk	
FILLING	
½ cup creamy peanut butter	
¾ cup confectioners' sugar	

Preheat oven to 350°F. Lightly grease a 9-inch pie pan.

Blend all crust ingredients together in a bowl with a spoon and press into prepared pan. Bake 8 to 10 minutes or until brown. Remove and allow to cool.

For filling, using a fork, mix peanut butter and confectioners' sugar until crumbly. Sprinkle peanut butter mixture into bottom of baked pie shell, reserving 2 tablespoons for garnish. Beat pudding mix with milk for 2 minutes, using a handheld electric mixer. Pour on top of peanut butter mixture. Spread with whipped topping. Sprinkle with remaining 2 tablespoons peanut butter mixture. Refrigerate several hours before serving.

SERVES 6 TO 8

Lauren's Chocolate Drizzle Pie

A DOLLOP OF FRESH sweetened whipped cream on a slice of this pie is a nice bonus!

1 Pillsbury refrigerated pie crust (15-ounce box contains 2 crusts)	1 15.5-ounce Pillsbury Thick 'n Fudgy Deluxe Brownie Mix
1 8-ounce package cream cheese, softened	¼ cup vegetable oil
3 tablespoons sugar	3 tablespoons water
1 teaspoon pure vanilla extract	½ cup semisweet chocolate chips
2 eggs	½ cup chopped pecans
	¼ cup Smucker's Dove milk chocolate ice cream topping

Preheat oven to 350°F.

Follow manufacturer's instruction for setting pie crust in pan. I recommend a deep dish.

Combine cream cheese, sugar, vanilla, and 1 egg in a bowl. Beat with a handheld electric mixer until smooth and set aside. In a large bowl, mix brownie mix, 1 egg, oil, and water. Beat 50 strokes. Spread half of brownie mixture into raw pie shell. Carefully spread cream cheese mixture over brownie layer. Sprinkle chocolate chips over cream cheese layer; top with remaining brownie mixture and sprinkle nuts on top. Bake for 40 to 50 minutes or until center puffs and crust is brown. Warm sauce slightly in microwave. Serve warm or at room temperature over pie.

SERVES 6 TO 8

Frozen Peach Pie Filling

GEORGIA IS KNOWN *as the Peach State. As far back as I can remember, young women have been referred to as "Georgia Peaches." The peaches that we grow are so unbelievably good, but as with any other fresh crop, the harvest season comes and goes before you know it. This is a great way to serve your family fresh peach pies all year-round.*

9 pounds fresh peaches	3½ cups sugar
2 teaspoons Fruit Fresh (a preservative that prevents fruit from turning dark; found in the canning section at your grocery store)	½ cup plus 2 tablespoons quick-cooking tapioca
	¼ cup fresh lemon juice
	1 teaspoon salt

Peel, halve, pit, and slice peaches and put in a bowl. Stir together Fruit Fresh and sugar, then stir into peaches. Stir in remaining ingredients. Line 4 pie pans with heavy foil or freezer paper, placing a piece of plastic wrap over foil. Let lining (foil and plastic) extend 5 inches over edges of pie pans. Put 4 to 5 cups filling in each pan. Loosely fold wrapping around pie; freeze until firm. When filling is frozen solid, remove from pans and wrap tightly. Return to freezer until ready to use.

On pie-baking day, simply pop frozen pie filling into a pastry-lined pan, dot with butter, and sprinkle with nutmeg or cinnamon. Top with an additional pastry crust and seal well. Bake at 400°F for 50 to 60 minutes or until juices begin to bubble through the crust. If you feel the pie crust is browning too fast, lower temperature to suit your oven, possibly to between 350° and 375°F.

To peel peaches the easy way, notch the end of each peach with an X. Using a paring knife, cut only into the skin, not the flesh of the fruit. Gently drop fruit into rapidly boiling water. The ripeness of the peaches will determine how long to leave them in the water; usually 30 seconds to a minute is sufficient. You will see the skin loosening where you made the X. Remove fruit with a slotted spoon and plunge into a bowl of ice water; leave for about a minute. The skin should slip off easily. If not, return fruit to boiling water for an additional 30 seconds.

SERVES 6 TO 8

Georgia Cracker Pie

THIS YUMMY PIE *is best served chilled.*

¾ cup saltine crackers, finely crushed	½ cup chopped nuts
1 cup sugar, plus ¼ cup	1 teaspoon pure almond extract
½ teaspoon baking powder	3 egg whites at room temperature, stiffly beaten
12 dates, chopped	1 cup heavy cream

Preheat oven to 350°F. Generously grease a 9-inch pie pan.

Stir together crackers, the 1 cup sugar, baking powder, dates, nuts, and almond in a bowl. Fold in stiffly beaten egg whites. Pour into prepared pan. Bake for 30 minutes. Serve pie chilled. Whip cream with the ¼ cup sugar until peaks form. Just before serving, spread top of pie with fresh sweetened whipped cream.

SERVES 6 TO 8

Green Tomato Pie

This goes to show a southerner will make a pie out of just about anything.

CRUST

2 cups all-purpose flour

¼ teaspoon salt

1 teaspoon sugar

1 teaspoon baking powder

¾ cup butter-flavored Crisco

½ cup cold water

FILLING

4 to 5 green tomatoes, or enough to fill pie crust, thinly sliced

1¼ cups sugar

2 tablespoons Minute Tapioca

1 teaspoon grated lemon or orange zest

½ teaspoon ground cinnamon

¼ teaspoon freshly grated nutmeg

½ cup raisins (optional)

4 teaspoons butter, chopped into small pieces

GLAZE

1 tablespoon milk or 1 slightly beaten egg white

Sugar, for sprinkling

Sift together flour, salt, sugar, and baking powder into a bowl. Cut Crisco into flour mixture with a pastry cutter or fork until mixture resembles corn meal. Stir in ¼ cup of the cold water, then add remaining ¼ cup. Cover dough and allow it to rest in refrigerator for 30 minutes.

Preheat oven to 350°F.

Divide dough in half. Place on lightly floured board and pat out. Using a rolling pin, roll dough to the size of a 9-inch pie pan. Put crust in pan and trim off excess dough around the edge.

Put tomato slices in pie crust. Mix sugar, tapioca, zest, cinnamon, nutmeg, and raisins (if using) together and sprinkle over tomatoes. Dot with butter. Roll out remaining dough. Gently lay dough over filling, tucking any extra under bottom crust. Flute edges by pinching dough with your fingers, or using the wrong end of a butter knife, to give crust a decorative finish. Using a sharp knife, make 4 to 6 slits in top of crust to allow steam to escape. Brush top with a small amount of milk or an egg white. Sprinkle top with a little sugar to give your crust a shine.

Place pie in oven, and increase heat at once to 425°F. Bake for 25 minutes. Reduce temperature to 350°F and continue to bake for 20 more minutes. (If your pie looks ready to "spew out," open oven door for about 2 minutes.) Cool on wire rack.

SERVES 6 TO 8

Grits Pie

I KNOW A LOT of y'all who are reading this cookbook have probably never eaten grits. But down south, it's truly a staple in our cabinets. In fact, it's said down here that "grits" stands for Girls Raised In The South. Considering how attached we are to our grits, a southern cookbook from a southern girl just wouldn't be complete without a grits recipe in it somewhere, even a dessert book. Please do yourself a favor and make this pie. It'll make you sass your mama!

1 unbaked 9-inch pie shell	2 tablespoons all-purpose flour
¾ cup water	2 eggs, slightly beaten
⅛ teaspoon salt	¼ cup buttermilk
¼ cup quick-cooking grits	1 teaspoon pure vanilla extract
½ cup (1 stick) butter	Freshly ground nutmeg (optional)
¾ cup sugar	

Prepare your crust and set aside.

Preheat oven to 325°F.

In a small saucepan, bring water and salt to a boil. Add grits and cook for 4 minutes. It's not especially easy to cook such a small amount of grits, so this will require your constant attention. Stir almost entire time that the grits are cooking. Add butter and continue to cook and stir for an additional minute. Set aside. In a bowl, stir together sugar, flour, eggs, buttermilk, and vanilla. Stir into cooked grits. Pour into pie shell and bake for 35 to 40 minutes or until set. This pie is delicious warm or cold. If desired, serve with a dollop of fresh sweetened whipped cream and a strawberry for garnish, and blow your guests away, girls and boys.

Before baking the pie, you may sprinkle with freshly ground nutmeg. This will give it a taste much like egg custard pie. I personally love the pie plain, with just the pure wonderful flavor of grits coming through.

SERVES 6 TO 8

Key Lime Grits Pie

I HAD JUST TAKEN a grits pie out of the oven when a friend walked in. A piece was immediately shoved in his face and I asked, "What kind of pie is this?"

After he'd made a couple of wrong guesses, I finally confessed to him that he was enjoying a grits pie. His face lit up, and he said, "You know what I think, Paula? I think this would make a wonderful Key lime pie."

"You know, J.R.," I said, "you just might be right." So back to the stove I went. If I say so myself, the results are pretty good.

1 unbaked deep-dish 9-inch pie shell	¼ cup buttermilk
1 cup water	⅓ cup fresh Key lime juice (use bottled if fresh limes are unavailable)
⅛ teaspoon salt	
⅓ cup quick-cooking grits	
½ cup (1 stick) butter	MERINGUE
1 cup sugar	3 egg whites
2 tablespoons all-purpose flour	¼ teaspoon cream of tartar
3 egg yolks, slightly beaten	6 tablespoons sugar

Prepare your crust and set aside.

Preheat oven to 325°F.

In a small saucepan, bring water and salt to a boil. Add grits and cook for 4 minutes. It's not especially easy to cook such a small amount of grits, so this will require your constant attention. Stir almost entire time that the grits are cooking. Add butter and continue to cook and stir for an additional minute. Set aside.

In a bowl, stir together sugar, flour, egg yolks, buttermilk, and Key lime juice. Stir into cooked grits. Pour into pie shell and bake for 35 to 40 minutes or until set. Remove pie from oven.

Prepare meringue by beating egg whites and cream of tartar together until frothy. Continue to beat until soft peaks form. Slowly add sugar and beat until stiff but not dry. Spread over top of pie, sealing edges well. (Meringue should touch the edges of crust. Meringue can shrink up and come loose from crust if it is not sealed well.) Increase oven temperature to 350°F and bake for 10 to 12 minutes or until meringue is a golden brown. This pie is delicious warm or cold.

SERVES 6 TO 8

John Berendt's Favorite Angel Pie

SAVANNAH, GEORGIA, *from the very beginning, has always been a beautiful and mysterious place, with the ability to capture people's hearts and minds, and so has always had her share of tourism. But for recent revitalization, rekindled interest, and tourism growth, John Berendt, in my opinion, has to be placed at the forefront.* Midnight in the Garden of Good and Evil, *his dark, southern gothic account of a not-so-reputable side of Savannah, reawakened the appetite of the country for more knowledge about our city, her personality, and the lives lived here.*

I had the pleasure of meeting John while I was writing my first cookbook, The Lady & Sons Savannah Country Cookbook. *It was a real honor he bestowed on me by writing the foreword for that book. His mother, Carol Berendt, is a kind and gracious lady happy to share with me the dishes John loves so much. This happens to be one of them. John says, "I could eat that all day." I think you'll feel the same way when you taste John's Favorite Angel Pie.*

MERINGUE	FILLING
4 egg whites, at room temperature	3 1-ounce squares unsweetened chocolate
1⅓ cups sugar	4 egg yolks
2 teaspoons cornstarch	½ cup sugar
2 teaspoons white vinegar	⅛ teaspoon salt
¾ teaspoon pure vanilla extract	2 tablespoons water
	1 cup heavy cream, whipped

Preheat oven to 450°F. Grease a 9- or 10-inch pie pan.

For meringue, beat egg whites with a handheld electric mixer until soft peaks form. Stir together sugar and cornstarch in a bowl, then add 2 tablespoons at a time to egg whites, beating well between additions. After third addition, beat in vinegar. Before last addition, beat in vanilla. Turn into prepared pan, pushing tightly against sides to form a pie crust. Place in oven and turn off oven heat. Leave pie in oven at least 3 hours.

For filling, melt chocolate in top of a double boiler. In a bowl, beat yolks, sugar, salt, and water thoroughly; stir mixture into melted chocolate. Cook over boiling water, stirring constantly until very thick (don't let top pan touch the water). Cool completely. Fold chocolate mixture into whipped cream. Pour into cooled shell; chill overnight.

SERVES 6 TO 8

Lemon Birdie Pie

*This **definitely** is **not** your run-of-the-mill lemon pie, y'all!*

FILLING

1 cup sugar

3 tablespoons cornstarch

1 cup milk

3 egg yolks, beaten

¼ cup (½ stick) butter

¼ cup lemon juice

1 8-ounce carton sour cream

1 9-inch graham cracker pie shell

MERINGUE

3 egg whites, at room temperature

½ teaspoon pure vanilla extract

6 tablespoons sugar

Preheat oven to 350°F.

Mix together sugar and cornstarch in a saucepan; slowly stir in milk. Over medium heat, cook mixture until thick, stirring constantly. Remove from heat. Pour small amount of sugar-milk mixture into egg yolks (this process is referred to as "tempering" and will prevent you from having chunks of cooked eggs in your custard). Mix well and slowly return to hot sugar-milk mixture. Return to heat, bring to a light boil, and continue to cook for 2 minutes, stirring constantly. Remove from heat. Add butter and lemon juice. Cool completely. Fold in sour cream and pour into pie shell.

For meringue, put egg whites and vanilla in a deep narrow bowl. Beat with a handheld electric mixer until frothy. Adding 1 tablespoon of sugar at a time, continue to beat until stiff peaks form. Spread over top of pie, sealing edges well. Bake for 10 to 12 minutes or until meringue is golden brown.

SERVES 6

Lemon Chess Pie

CHESS PIES REQUIRE *few ingredients, which probably accounted for their popularity here in the Deep South so many years ago. I know for a fact that this particular recipe is at least sixty years old, and I would like to give it to you much as it was written.*

2 cups sugar	¼ cup (½ stick) butter, melted
Good pinch of salt	¼ cup milk
1 tablespoon water-ground white or yellow cornmeal	Grated zest and juice of 2 lemons
1 tablespoon flour	4 eggs
	1 unbaked 9-inch pie shell

Preheat oven to 350°F.

Mix sugar, salt, cornmeal, and flour in a fair-sized bowl. Mix in melted butter that you have heated a bit and add milk. Add grated zest of lemons and lemon juice to sugar mixture. Toss in eggs, beat like mad for a minute or so, and you will be ready to pour this elegant mixture into a pie shell.

But wait one small minute while you run this unbaked shell under the red-hot broiler for 60 seconds. This will do wonders for the crust (put this dandy tip in the back of your hat for future reference, in case you ever make any other kind of pie). Bake for about 40 minutes. You had better peek after a half hour to be sure all is well and the lovely brown delicate crust that forms on top is tanning to perfection. The center should be just barely firm, so don't overbake, please.

SERVES 6

Sean Jones Sweet Potato Pie

ONE DAY THIS BIG TALL *strapping man walked into The Lady & Sons to enjoy the lunch buffet. I didn't know him, but you can't help but notice a man when he cuts the figure that this man did.*

Jamie and Bobby came over and said to me, "Mom, that's Sean Jones." My reply was "That's wonderful. Who's Sean Jones?" And they both just looked at me like I was from outer space.

Indignant, they said, "Mother, he's the all-pro defensive end for the Packers!"

"Great," I said. "What's the Packers?"

Disgust was written all over their faces. "Football, Mom, football. Remember? You were a cheerleader! You know, 'rah-rah,' and all that stuff."

Jamie and Bobby wanted to meet Mr. Jones but they said, "He's not smiling much." Why ain't he smiling? He's eating some good groceries. So I go to find out. I had a great conversation with him and his lunch companion. I asked what his favorite dessert was. With a smile, he said, "Oh, it's gotta be sweet potato pie."

"Well, Sean, I tell ya what," I said. "I'm writing a dessert cookbook, and I'm going to formulate a sweet potato pie recipe just for you."

Betcha thought you'd never hear about that recipe, didn't you, Sean? Well, here it is, and it's pretty darned good!

4 ounces cream cheese, softened	½ teaspoon ground cinnamon
2 cups mashed sweet potatoes	1 teaspoon pure vanilla extract
1¼ cups sugar	1 unbaked deep-dish 9-inch
¼ cup half-and-half	pie shell
¼ cup (½ stick) butter, melted	Whipped cream, for garnish
2 eggs, slightly beaten	

Preheat oven to 350°F.

In bowl of an electric mixer, beat cream cheese and sweet potatoes together. Add sugar and half-and-half; continue to beat until mixture is fluffy. Add butter and eggs; mix well. Toss in cinnamon and vanilla, again mixing well. Pour into unbaked pie shell. Bake in center of oven for 50 to 60 minutes or until set. Serve with a dollop of fresh whipped cream. Hope you love it, Sean!

🌿 *You may use canned sweet potatoes if you like, but personally I don't ever use anything but fresh. Just throw the potatoes in the oven and bake until done or cook in the microwave. Or, if you have any leftover sweet potatoes from last night's dinner, this is a great way to use them up. Peel and mash.*

SERVES 1 SEAN JONES OR 6 TO 8

Sin-sational Pie

This is just sinful!

2 unbaked deep-dish 9-inch pie shells	¼ cup (½ stick) butter
1 8-ounce package cream cheese, softened	1 7-ounce can sweetened coconut
1 14-ounce can sweetened condensed milk	1 cup chopped pecans
1 16-ounce container whipped topping	1 12-ounce jar caramel ice cream topping

Bake pie shells according to package directions. In a bowl, beat together cream cheese and condensed milk with a handheld electric mixer until smooth; fold in whipped topping. Melt butter in a skillet, add coconut and pecans, and toast until golden brown, stirring constantly. Heat caramel topping slightly in microwave or on stove over low heat, until pouring consistency is achieved. In cooled pie shell, layer in this order: cream cheese mixture, coconut-pecan mixture, then caramel topping, drizzled on for final layer.

SERVES 12 TO 16

Snickers Pie

THIS IS JUST TOO GOOD *and too simple!*

For a richer pie, substitute 2 cups heavy cream, whipped with ½ cup sugar until stiff peaks form, in place of prepared whipped topping.

4 king-sized Snickers bars

½ cup peanut butter

1½ tablespoons half-and-half

4 cups frozen whipped topping, thawed

1 deep-dish 9-inch graham cracker pie crust

Additional whipped topping and Hershey's chocolate syrup, for garnish

In the top of a double boiler, melt together Snickers bars, peanut butter, and half-and-half, stirring until smooth. Remove from heat and allow to cool slightly. Fold in whipped topping, pour into crust, and freeze for 4 to 6 hours before serving. When ready to serve, top with additional whipped topping and drizzle with Hershey's chocolate syrup. Store in refrigerator.

SERVES 6 TO 8

White Chocolate Macadamia Nut Pie

ANOTHER FABULOUS *Gabriel's Desserts recipe. Thank you, Cuz.*

GANACHE

¾ cup semisweet chocolate
   chips

½ cup heavy cream

FILLING

6½ ounces cream cheese, softened

2½ cups granulated sugar

⅓ cup heavy cream, plus ¾ cup,
   whipped soft

6½ 1-ounce squares Baker's
   premium white chocolate,
   melted

½ teaspoon orange zest

⅔ cup roasted chopped
   macadamia nuts

1 pre-baked deep-dish 9-inch
   pie shell

GARNISH

1½ cups heavy cream

¼ cup confectioners' sugar

1 to 2 ounces chopped
   macadamia nuts

For ganache, put chocolate chips in a metal mixing bowl. Bring cream to a light boil and pour over chips until they completely dissolve. Set aside and allow to cool to room temperature.

For filling, beat cream cheese and granulated sugar with a handheld electric mixer until smooth. Scrape bowl with a spatula and mix in the ⅓ cup heavy cream. Add the white chocolate, zest, and nuts and stir just until incorporated. Fold in the ¾ cup heavy cream. Spread into pre-baked pie shell and level off using a rubber spatula. Put in freezer until frozen. To finish pie, you will need to place the ganache in a microwave on the low setting for no more than 10 seconds at a time. Stir after each warming until ganache pours loosely but is not even close to boiling (see note). Spread warm ganache over top of frozen pie, smoothing to the edges with a spatula.

For garnish, beat cream and confectioners' sugar with a handheld electric mixer to a stiff peak. Pipe edges of pie with whipped cream. Sprinkle macadamia nuts over pie. Store pie in refrigerator.

🌿 *Be very careful when warming chocolate, as it will burn very quickly when heated in the microwave. Once chocolate is scorched it is unusable.*

SERVES 6 TO 8

Cookies & Bars

Gooey Butter Cakes ✤ Brown Sugar Squares ✤ Chocolate Meringue
Kisses ✤ Coconut Pecan Bars ✤ Cream Cheese Cookies ✤
Date-Nut Sticks ✤ Frosted Pumpkin Bars ✤ Hidden Mint
Cookies ✤ Iron Skillet Brownies ✤ Molasses Cookies ✤ Oatmeal-
Chip Cookies ✤ Orange Brownies ✤ Paula's Loaded Oatmeal
Cookies ✤ Peanut Butter Bars ✤ Pecan Dreams ✤ Pecan
Shortbread Bars ✤ Praline Cookies ✤ Savannah Cheesecake
Cookies ✤ Stick to Your Teeth Chocolate Cookies ✤ Willie Wonder
Wafers ✤ Marble Cheesecake Bars ✤ Two Brothers' Chocolate Gobs

Helpful Hints

1. Begin with a good, heavy cookie sheet. Dark cookie sheets can produce a dark, almost burned bottom. Always keep two good baking sheets in your kitchen inventory. You will be able to keep a constant flow of cookies going into the oven. This will also allow the pans to cool in between batches of cookies. Never put cookie dough on a really hot pan.

2. Be consistent in the size you make your cookies.

3. Place cookie sheet on the center rack of the oven.

4. Because most ovens have "hot spots," you may find that one side is browning faster than the other. Simply give the pan a 180-degree turn halfway into cooking time, placing what was the front of the pan in the rear.

5. If your cookies are coming out too flat, you might try adding a little more flour. If that doesn't work, try chilling the dough in the refrigerator.

6. If you don't have a cooling rack, transfer cookies to a waxed paper–lined surface to cool.

7. I find that a thin metal spatula works better than a thick plastic spatula for removing cookies from the pan.

8. Store cookies in an airtight container instead of a cookie jar for a longer shelf life. If it's a sticky cookie, place a sheet of waxed paper between the layers of cookies. I don't like to use a cookie tin except to transfer from one location to another for a short period of time.

9. For crisp cookies that have gone soft, place on a cookie sheet into a low oven (225° to 250°F) for a few minutes.

10. To keep a soft cookie from staling, throw a piece of bread in the container along with the cookie. A slice of apple works great also. I remember when I was a child my mother throwing in an apple wedge with her Christmas fruitcakes to keep them moist.

11. If you like a dense cookie, mix by hand. If you prefer a lighter, crisper cookie, beat with an electric mixer. This will put more air into the dough.

12. Parchment paper is a great pan saver. If cut to fit the baking sheet, it eliminates greasing the pan and cleanup.

13. Adjust your baking time on cookies to suit your taste. If you like a softer, chewy cookie, cut back on cooking time. If you like a crisper cookie, increase cooking time.

Gooey Butter Cakes

Butter Gooey Cakes. Ooey Gooey Butter Cakes. Ooey Booey Gooey Cakes. These are just a few of the names I've heard our guests at The Lady & Sons call 'em. But to quote Shakespeare:

What's in a name? that which we call a rose
By any other name would smell as sweet.

This is exactly how I feel about our Gooey Butter Cakes. No matter what you call them, they're like that sweet rose that Shakespeare wrote about. These delectable cakes were an instant hit the first day they showed up in The Bag Lady basket and they immediately became one of my most requested items. These little sweeties actually resemble a bar-type dessert instead of what we know as a traditional cake. Over the years, I have made every flavor imaginable, using this basic recipe. I'll give you some of my recommendations but by all means experiment and have fun creating your very own version of our signature Gooey Butter Cakes.

CAKE	2 eggs
1 18.25-ounce box yellow cake mix	1 teaspoon pure vanilla extract
1 egg	1 16-ounce box confectioners'
½ cup (1 stick) butter, melted	sugar
FILLING	½ cup (1 stick) butter, melted
1 8-ounce package cream cheese, softened	

Preheat oven to 350°F. Lightly grease a 13 × 9 × 2-inch baking pan.

In the bowl of an electric mixer, combine cake mix, egg, and butter and mix well. Pat into the bottom of prepared pan and set aside. Still using an electric mixer, beat cream cheese until smooth; add eggs and vanilla. Dump in confectioners' sugar and beat well. Reduce speed of mixer and slowly pour in butter. Mix well. Pour filling onto cake mixture and spread evenly. Bake for 40 to 50 minutes. Don't be afraid to make a judgment call on the cooking time, because oven temperatures can vary. You want the center to be a little gooey, so don't bake it past that point! Remove from oven and allow to cool completely. Cut into squares. Just remember that these wonderful little cakes are very, very rich, and a little will go a long way—even for piggies like me!

PUMPKIN GOOEY: This variation has to be at the top of my list, especially around Thanksgiving. For the cake part, I sometimes use a spice cake mix. I have even used a chocolate cake mix, but I think my favorite is the basic yellow cake mix. Follow the original recipe, adding a 15-ounce can of pumpkin pie filling and an extra egg to the cream cheese filling. Bake as usual, remove from oven, and allow to cool. Cut into squares and top each square with a pecan half. Serve with a dollop of fresh whipped cream. I promise you'll never want pumpkin pie again!

PINEAPPLE GOOEY: Add a 20-ounce can of drained crushed pineapple and an extra egg to the cream cheese filling. Proceed as directed above.

LEMON GOOEY: Use a lemon cake mix in place of the yellow cake. Add the juice (approximately ¼ cup) and zest of 2 lemons to the cream cheese filling. Proceed as directed above.

CARROT CAKE GOOEY: Use a spice cake mix, and add 1 cup chopped nuts and 1½ cups finely grated carrots to the cream cheese filling. Proceed as directed above.

PEANUT BUTTER GOOEY: Use a chocolate cake mix. Add 1 cup creamy peanut butter and an extra egg to cream cheese filling. You can sprinkle the top of batter with 1 cup chopped peanuts if you like. Proceed as directed above.

CHOCOLATE CHIP GOOEY: Use either yellow or chocolate cake mix. Sprinkle 1 cup chocolate chips and 1 cup chopped nuts on top of filling. Proceed as directed above.

BANANA GOOEY: Use a yellow cake mix. Prepare cream cheese filling as directed, beating in 2 ripe bananas and an extra egg. Proceed as directed above.

NUTTY GOOEY: Use a yellow cake mix, and add 1 cup chopped nuts to the cake mixture. Proceed as directed above.

CHIPPY GOOEY: Stir 1 cup white chocolate chips, peanut butter chocolate chips, butterscotch morsels, Heath Almond Toffee Bits or Heath Milk Chocolate Toffee Bits into filling. Proceed as directed above.

YIELDS 20 TO 24 SQUARES

Brown Sugar Squares

THESE ARE EASY *and delicious and don't require a mixer, just a bowl and spoon.*

1 egg	¼ teaspoon baking soda
1 cup light brown sugar	¼ teaspoon salt
1 teaspoon pure vanilla extract	1 cup chopped nuts
½ cup all-purpose flour	

Preheat oven to 350°F. Grease an 8-inch square pan.

Stir together egg, sugar, and vanilla in a bowl. Sift together flour, soda, and salt in another bowl. Quickly stir into egg mixture. Add nuts and spread in pan. Bake for 18 to 20 minutes. Cookies should be soft in center. Cut into squares.

YIELDS 16 2-INCH SQUARES

Chocolate Meringue Kisses

YOU KNOW, *as this recipe was being tested I became acutely aware of how important instructions are for the cook, even for the simplest recipes.*

My brother Bubba is comptroller at our restaurant. He is the father of my pride and joy, Corrie Hiers. She was working in the office at The Lady & Sons and occasionally she would come out to my house after work to see if I needed help with anything.

One afternoon I stuck this recipe into her hand and said, "Puddin' Head, how about testing this recipe for me." I didn't say another word because I thought it was self-explanatory. Boy, was I wrong. After thirty minutes of hearing her rattling around, I got up from the computer to check her progress.

She was on her ninth egg white, and you'll notice the recipe only calls for three. There were eggshells everywhere, and Corrie had a firm grip on the bowl as she beat the devil out of those egg whites with a wire whisk. She'd already tried a fork and given up. For some reason they just wouldn't get stiff. Imagine that.

I laughed and said, "Corrie, don't you know that has to be done with an electric mixer?" She turned to me and said, "No, Aunt Paula, it didn't say that in the directions."

By the way, she finally produced a perfect batch of chocolate meringue kisses that literally melted in your mouth.

1 cup confectioners' sugar

3 egg whites, stiffly beaten (*please* use an electric mixer)

½ cup crushed saltine crackers

½ cup chopped walnuts or pecans

1 teaspoon pure vanilla extract

1 6-ounce package semisweet chocolate chips

Preheat oven to 325°F. Grease a cookie sheet.

In a bowl, fold confectioners' sugar into stiffly beaten egg whites a little at a time. Fold in crackers, nuts, and vanilla. Melt chocolate in a double boiler over hot water and allow to cool slightly. Fold into egg white mixture. Drop by rounded half teaspoonfuls onto greased cookie sheet. Bake for 12 minutes. Remove cookies from oven. Repeat until all dough has been used.

YIELDS 4 DOZEN KISSES

Coconut Pecan Bars

½ teaspoon salt	½ teaspoon baking powder
1½ cups light brown sugar	1½ cups flaked, sweetened coconut
1 cup all-purpose flour, plus 2 tablespoons	1 cup chopped pecans
½ cup (1 stick) butter, softened	1 15-ounce container Duncan Hines Creamy Home-Style Coconut Pecan Frosting
1 teaspoon pure vanilla extract	
2 eggs, well beaten	

Preheat oven to 325°F.

For first layer, combine salt, ½ cup of the sugar, and the 1 cup flour in a bowl. Cut butter into flour mixture, using a fork or pastry cutter, until it resembles meal. Pat into bottom of an 8 × 2-inch square pan. Bake about 25 minutes or until slightly brown. While first layer is baking, blend together in a bowl remaining 1 cup sugar, vanilla, eggs, the 2 tablespoons flour, baking powder, coconut, and pecans. When first layer is done, remove from oven and very carefully spread coconut mixture over crust without disturbing crust. Return to oven and continue to bake about 25 minutes, or until set. Remove from oven and allow to cool completely. Spread coconut pecan frosting over top; slice into bars.

YIELDS 28 SQUARES

Cream Cheese Cookies

1 cup (2 sticks) butter, softened	2 egg yolks
1 3-ounce package cream cheese, softened	½ teaspoon pure vanilla extract
1 cup sugar	2½ cups all-purpose flour

Cream together butter and cream cheese, using an electric mixer; add sugar and beat until fluffy. Add egg yolks and vanilla. Add flour, stirring, ½ cup at a time. Chill dough for 30 minutes.

Preheat oven to 350° and grease one or more cookie sheets. Roll dough out to ¼ inch thick; cut with cookie cutters. Place cookies on a cookie sheet and bake for 10 to 12 minutes. Cool and serve.

YIELDS ABOUT 4 DOZEN COOKIES

Date-Nut Sticks

A TRAY OF GOODIES at Christmastime is not complete without these. It's one of my family's favorites.

¾ cup (1½ sticks) butter	2 teaspoons pure vanilla extract
2 eggs, beaten	1 cup chopped nuts
2 cups sugar	1½ cups Rice Crispies
1 8-ounce box chopped dates	3 cups finely grated coconut

In a saucepan over medium heat, melt butter. Add eggs, sugar, and dates. Bring to a boil, reduce heat to low, and cook 10 minutes, stirring constantly. Remove from heat. Stir in vanilla, nuts, and Rice Crispies. Cool and shape into finger-sized sticks. Roll in coconut.

YIELDS 45 STICKS

Frosted Pumpkin Bars

BARS	1 teaspoon salt
4 large eggs	1 teaspoon baking soda
1⅔ cups granulated sugar	
1 cup corn oil	ICING
1 16-ounce can pumpkin	1 3-ounce package cream cheese, softened
2 cups all-purpose flour	½ cup (1 stick) butter, softened
2 teaspoons baking powder	1 teaspoon pure vanilla extract
1 teaspoon cinnamon	2 cups sifted confectioners' sugar

Preheat oven to 350°F.

In bowl of an electric mixer, beat eggs, granulated sugar, oil, and pumpkin until fluffy. Sift together flour, baking powder, cinnamon, salt, and baking soda in another bowl. Gradually add to the egg mixture with the mixer at low speed. Spread batter in an ungreased 15 × 10 × 1-inch jelly roll pan. Bake for 20 to 25 minutes or until center of cake is done. Remove from oven and cool completely.

For icing, cream together cream cheese and butter with an electric mixer; add vanilla. Slowly beat in confectioners' sugar until smooth. Frost cake with icing and cut into squares. These freeze well.

YIELDS 24 BARS

Hidden Mint Cookies

ANTHONY, MICHAEL'S SON, *loved these cookies the first time I baked them for him to take back to military school. After showing him how simple they were to make, more often than not, Anthony is the one in the kitchen doing the baking now.*

1 18-ounce roll refrigerated Pillsbury Sugar Cookies, sliced thin	1 tablespoon coarsely chopped walnuts or pecans, or enough to cover top of cookies
1 package chocolate mint wafers	

Preheat oven to 375°F. Slightly grease a cookie sheet.

Place slices of sugar cookies on sheet. Top each with a chocolate wafer. Cover wafer with another slice of cookie dough. Press nuts into top of dough. Bake for about 10 minutes.

YIELDS ABOUT 20 COOKIES

Iron Skillet Brownies

2 1-ounce squares unsweetened chocolate	2 teaspoons pure vanilla extract
½ cup (1 stick) butter	¼ cup unbleached flour
1 cup sugar	¼ teaspoon salt
2 eggs	1 cup chopped pecans

Preheat oven to 325°F. Grease an 8 × 2-inch square pan.

Melt chocolate and butter in an iron skillet over medium heat; stir to prevent scorching. Remove from heat and stir in sugar. Add eggs and vanilla; stir in flour, salt, and pecans. Mix well. Pour into prepared pan. Bake for 40 minutes. Let cool and cut into squares.

YIELDS 9 LARGE OR 16 SMALL SQUARES

Molasses Cookies

1 cup light brown sugar	2 teaspoons cinnamon
1 cup unsulfured molasses	1 teaspoon ground ginger
1 cup vegetable shortening, melted	½ teaspoon cloves
	2 teaspoons baking soda
2 eggs, beaten	1 cup boiling water
4 cups all-purpose flour	1 cup raisins

Preheat oven to 375°F. Grease one or more cookie sheets.

Mix together sugar, molasses, and shortening in a bowl. Stir in eggs. Sift together flour, cinnamon, ginger, and cloves in another bowl. Add baking soda to boiling water in a saucepan. Add water and flour mixtures alternately to sugar mixture, beginning and ending with flour. Stir in raisins. Drop batter by teaspoons onto cookie sheet. Bake for 8 to 10 minutes.

YIELDS ABOUT 6 DOZEN COOKIES

Oatmeal-Chip Cookies

1 cup (2 sticks) butter, softened	1 teaspoon baking powder
1 cup sugar	1 teaspoon baking soda
1 cup light brown sugar	1 12-ounce package semisweet chocolate chips
2 eggs, beaten	
1 teaspoon pure vanilla extract	1 9-ounce Hershey Bar (milk chocolate), grated
2½ cups quick-cooking oatmeal	
2 cups all-purpose flour	1½ cups chopped nuts
½ teaspoon salt	

Preheat oven to 375°F. Lightly grease one or more cookie sheets.

Using an electric mixer, cream butter and sugars together in a bowl until fluffy. Add eggs one at a time, beating well after each addition. Add vanilla. In a food processor, blend oatmeal to a fine powder. Mix in a bowl with flour, salt, baking powder, and baking soda; add to creamed mixture. Mix well. Stir in chocolate chips, grated Hershey Bar, and nuts. Roll into balls and place 2 inches apart on cookie sheet. Bake for 10 minutes.

YIELDS ABOUT 4½ DOZEN COOKIES

Orange Brownies

I've had the opportunity to make so many new friends in the restaurant. Robin Wilson from Altamonte Springs, Florida, is one of those. Robin recently was one of a hundred finalists in the 39th Pillsbury Bake-Off, where she won a side-by-side refrigerator and a trip to San Francisco. As she and her husband were enjoying lunch at The Lady & Sons, she mentioned her Orange Brownies, and was happy to share the recipe. Thanks, Robin, and good luck to ya in your next bake-off! Get that gold, girl!

1½ cups all-purpose flour	GLAZE
2 cups granulated sugar	1 cup confectioners' sugar
1 teaspoon salt	2 tablespoons orange juice
1 cup (2 sticks) butter, softened	1 teaspoon grated orange zest
4 eggs	
2 teaspoons pure orange extract	
1 teaspoon grated orange zest	

Preheat oven to 350°F. Grease a 13 × 9 × 2-inch pan.

Stir together flour, granulated sugar, and salt in a bowl; add butter, eggs, extract, and zest. Using a handheld electric mixer, beat until well blended. Pour batter into prepared pan and bake for 30 minutes, or until light golden brown and set. Remove from oven and pierce entire cake with a fork.

For glaze, mix all ingredients together and stir until smooth. Pour glaze over cake. Cool and cut into squares.

YIELDS 24 SQUARES

Paula's Loaded Oatmeal Cookies

½ cup (1 stick) butter, softened

½ cup vegetable shortening

1½ cups packed light brown sugar

2 eggs

½ cup buttermilk

1¾ cups all-purpose flour

1 teaspoon baking soda

½ teaspoon salt

1 teaspoon baking powder

1 teaspoon ground ginger

1 teaspoon freshly ground
   nutmeg

1 teaspoon ground cinnamon

¼ teaspoon ground cloves

½ teaspoon ground allspice

2½ cups quick-cooking oatmeal

1 cup raisins

1½ cups chopped walnuts

1 teaspoon pure vanilla extract

Preheat oven to 350°F. Grease one or more cookie sheets.

Using an electric mixer, cream together butter, shortening, and sugar in a bowl until fluffy. Add eggs and beat until mixture is light in color. Add buttermilk. Sift together flour, baking soda, salt, baking powder, ginger, nutmeg, cinnamon, cloves, and allspice; stir into creamed mixture. Fold in oatmeal, raisins, walnuts, and vanilla, blending well. Drop by rounded teaspoons onto cookie sheet. Bake for 12 to 15 minutes.

YIELDS ABOUT 5 DOZEN COOKIES

Peanut Butter Bars

½ cup (1 stick) butter, softened

½ cup granulated sugar

½ cup light brown sugar

1 egg

⅓ cup creamy peanut butter

½ teaspoon baking soda

¼ teaspoon salt

1 cup all-purpose flour

½ teaspoon pure vanilla extract

1 cup quick-cooking oatmeal

ICING

1 16-ounce container Duncan Hines chocolate icing

2 tablespoons creamy peanut butter

Preheat oven to 375°F. Grease a 15 × 10 × 1-inch jelly roll pan.

Beat together butter and sugars with a handheld electric mixer until creamy. Add egg and beat well. Add peanut butter and beat until incorporated. Sift together baking soda, salt, and flour in another bowl. Stir into creamed mixture; add vanilla and stir in oats. Pour into prepared pan. Bake for 10 to 15 minutes. Cool briefly, then cover with chocolate icing mixed with peanut butter. Cut into finger lengths.

YIELDS ABOUT 2 DOZEN BARS

Pecan Dreams

Taste one of these and you'll see why we call them dreams!

1½ cups confectioners' sugar	TOPPING
1 cup all-purpose flour	1 cup heavy cream
1 8-ounce package cream cheese, at room temperature	2 tablespoons granulated sugar
½ cup (1 stick) butter, at room temperature	1 cup Heath Bits O' Brickle Toffee Bits
1 cup chopped pecans	

Preheat oven to 350°F. Lightly grease a 9 × 2-inch square pan.

Stir together confectioners' sugar and flour in a bowl. Using a pastry cutter or fork, cut cream cheese and butter into flour mixture until crumbly. Press mixture into prepared pan, distributing evenly. Pour nuts over mixture and press into dough. Bake for 30 minutes. Remove from oven and cool completely.

For topping, whip cream and granulated sugar together with a handheld electric mixer until stiff; fold in almond toffee bits. Spread over cake. Cut into squares. Store in refrigerator.

YIELDS 25 SMALL SQUARES

Pecan Shortbread Bars

Delicious!

¾ cup vegetable shortening	½ teaspoon pure vanilla extract
¾ cup confectioners' sugar	1 cup chopped pecans
1½ cups all-purpose flour, plus 2 tablespoons	GLAZE
1 cup packed light brown sugar	2 tablespoons butter, melted
½ teaspoon baking powder	1 tablespoon milk
¼ teaspoon salt	1 tablespoon rum or ½ teaspoon rum extract
2 eggs	1 cup confectioners' sugar

Preheat oven to 350°F.

Using a handheld electric mixer, cream shortening and confectioners' sugar together; blend in the 1½ cups flour on low speed. Press dough into bottom of an ungreased 13 × 9 × 2-inch pan. Bake for 12 to 15 minutes. While crust is baking, mix together brown sugar, the 2 tablespoons flour, baking powder, salt, eggs, vanilla, and pecans. Pour over hot crust, return to oven, and continue to bake for an additional 20 minutes.

For glaze, mix together ingredients and stir until smooth. Pour glaze over shortbread and allow to cool; cut into 2½-inch bars.

YIELDS 35 BARS

Praline Cookies

THESE COOKIES ARE NAMED *after the praline candies that Savannah is famous for because of their buttery brown sugar coating.*

24 graham crackers	1 cup packed light brown sugar
½ cup (1 stick) butter	1 cup chopped nuts
½ cup (1 stick) margarine	

Preheat oven to 350°F. Line a cookie sheet with aluminum foil.

Arrange graham crackers on foil, laying them as close together as possible. Snug foil up closely to edges of crackers. In a saucepan, mix butter, margarine, and sugar together, bring to a boil, and boil for 2 minutes. Stir nuts into hot mixture until well coated. Bake for 10 minutes. Remove from oven, and cut into strips, following the perforated lines on graham crackers.

YIELDS 48 PIECES

Savannah Cheesecake Cookies

THESE ARE A FAVORITE *among Savannahians.*

CRUST	FILLING
1 cup all-purpose flour	2 8-ounce packages cream cheese, softened
¼ cup packed light brown sugar	1 cup granulated sugar
1 cup chopped pecans	3 eggs
½ cup (1 stick) butter, melted	1 teaspoon pure vanilla or almond extract
	Fresh berries and mint leaves, for garnish

Preheat oven to 350°F.

Combine flour, brown sugar, pecans, and butter in a bowl. Press dough into an ungreased 13 × 9 × 2-inch pan. Bake for 12 to 15 minutes or until lightly browned.

For filling, beat cream cheese and granulated sugar together in a bowl until smooth, using a handheld electric mixer; add eggs and extract; beat well. Pour over crust. Bake for 20 minutes. Cool completely. Cut into squares before serving. Decorate tops with berries and mint leaves.

YIELDS 24 SQUARES

Stick to Your Teeth Chocolate Cookies

SEE IF YOU CAN GUESS *why I gave these wonderful cookies this name.*

2 1-ounce squares unsweetened chocolate	⅛ teaspoon salt
1 14-ounce can sweetened condensed milk	½ cup chopped walnuts
1 cup graham cracker crumbs, finely ground	1 teaspoon pure vanilla extract
	24 shelled walnut halves

Preheat oven to 350°F. Grease one or more cookie sheets.

Place the top pan of a double boiler over rapidly boiling water. Melt chocolate, add milk, and stir until mixture thickens, about 5 minutes. Remove from heat; add crumbs, salt, nuts, and vanilla. If the batter sits for very long it will get very stiff, so work quickly. Drop mixture by rounded teaspoons onto prepared cookie sheet. Place half a walnut on top of each cookie. Bake for 10 minutes. Remove cookies from sheet immediately onto waxed paper to cool.

YIELDS ABOUT 24 COOKIES

Willie Wonder Wafers

½ cup (1 stick) butter	1 teaspoon pure vanilla extract
1 cup packed light brown sugar	3 cups all-purpose flour
⅛ teaspoon salt	1 teaspoon baking powder
1 egg	

Cream together butter, sugar, salt, egg, and vanilla in a bowl until fluffy. Sift together flour and baking powder; gradually add to creamed mixture (dough will be very dry). Turn out onto a floured board and knead thoroughly until dough is well mixed and handles easily. Refrigerate overnight. To bake, preheat oven to 350°F and lightly grease one or more cookie sheets.

Roll dough into logs, slice thin, and place on cookie sheet. Bake for 8 to 10 minutes, watching very carefully that they don't burn. Cool and store.

YIELDS ABOUT 6 DOZEN WAFERS

Marble Cheesecake Bars

24 Oreo cookies, crushed	3 eggs, beaten
3 tablespoons butter, softened	1 teaspoon pure vanilla extract
3 8-ounce packages cream cheese, softened	2 1-ounce squares semisweet chocolate
1 14-ounce can sweetened condensed milk	¼ cup crème de cacao (optional)

Preheat oven to 300°F. Lightly spray a 13 × 9 × 2-inch pan with a nonstick coating.

Combine cookies and butter. Press cookie mixture into bottom of prepared pan. Beat cream cheese with a handheld electric mixer until fluffy; gradually beat in condensed milk. Add eggs and vanilla; mix well. Pour two thirds batter onto crust. Melt chocolate per package directions and add to remaining one third batter along with crème de cacao, if using. Spoon over top of vanilla layer. Draw a knife through to marbleize. Bake for 45 to 50 minutes or until set. Cool or chill; cut into bars. Store in refrigerator.

SERVES 16 TO 20

Two Brothers' Chocolate Gobs

I REMEMBER MAKING THESE so very often for two cute little towheaded brothers. If I shut my eyes I can see them right now, running through the back door, leading a pack of more cute little towheaded boys. They would be heading them straight to the refrigerator, slingin' open the door, laughin' and yappin' and wiping snot off their upper lips with their shirtsleeves, and smelling like wet dogs; the epitome of snips, and snails, and puppy-dog tails. The pack had interrupted their play long enough to come in and nab what they most assuredly knew would be in the bottom left-hand crisper drawer of the fridge: the yummy and unforgettable chocolate gob!

It's hard to believe that those two smelly little boys have grown into the same two handsome and good-smelling men: my dear sons, Jamie and Bobby Deen. And by the way, some things never change: after all these years, they still love those chocolate gobs.

CAKE	2 teaspoons baking soda
2 cups sugar	½ cup cocoa
½ cup vegetable shortening	
2 eggs	FILLING
1 cup buttermilk	5 tablespoons all-purpose flour
1 cup boiling water	1 cup milk
1 teaspoon pure vanilla extract	1 cup sugar
4 cups all-purpose flour	½ cup (1 stick) butter, softened
½ teaspoon baking powder	½ cup vegetable shortening
	1 teaspoon pure vanilla extract

Preheat oven to 425°F.

Cream together sugar and shortening in bowl of an electric mixer until fluffy; add eggs, continuing to beat. Stir together buttermilk, boiling water, and vanilla; blend this into creamed mixture at low speed. Sift together flour, baking powder, baking soda, and cocoa. Add to mixture 1 cup at a time, blending well at low speed. Batter will be very thin, but not to worry. Drop by teaspoons onto ungreased cookie sheet. Bake for 5 minutes, allow to cool, and transfer to wax paper.

For filling, put flour into a saucepan and slowly add milk, stirring until smooth. Set over medium heat and cook, stirring, until very thick. Remove from heat and allow to cool completely. Cream together sugar, butter, shortening, and vanilla with a handheld electric mixer. Add cooled flour mixture and whip until fluffy. Spread onto bottom side of cookie and top with another cookie, to make a sandwich. Wrap individually in plastic wrap, store in refrigerator, and save for those snotty-nosed precious little boys and girls.

YIELDS 25 GOBS

A One-Woman Show

PAULA DEEN

I HAVE SET SOME RULES for me and my staff concerning celebrity guests who dine at The Lady & Sons. We ask for no pictures or autographs unless they volunteer. We try to respect their privacy and treat them like any other guest.

Well, one Saturday night I almost broke my own rule when Ms. Bea Arthur of *The Golden Girls* walked into the restaurant. She was accompanied by her longtime friend Billy Goldenberg, the four-time Emmy-winning composer and pianist. Ms. Arthur was here in Savannah to perform her one-woman show, . . . *And Then There's Bea,* along with Mr. Goldenberg at the piano.

After they had been seated by the hostess, I walked over to welcome them and immediately turned into a blubbering idiot. I remember blurting out something like "I love you, girl!" As I was busy making a fool out of myself, she looked up at me, smiling, and simply said, "Thank you," but was probably saying to herself, "What is this babbling idiot saying?"

After I'd gained my composure we began talking about food. Bea said she definitely wanted to try our fried green tomatoes, and proceeded to tell me that she serves them quite often at her dinner parties. She went on to tell me how she prepares them. So I said to her, "Great. I'll have the kitchen prepare half of them your way and half of them our way." I must say, her way was absolutely delicious, giving a whole new twist to the fried green tomato. Hopefully one day I will have the opportunity in another book to share her recipe with y'all.

Puddings & Custards

Cassata Cake ❧ Eggnog Pudding ❧ Grape-Nuts Pudding ❧
Hazelnut Angel ❧ Lemon Curd Pudding ❧ Marvin's Banana Cream
Pie ❧ Not Yo' Mama's Banana Pudding ❧ The Lady & Sons' Peach
Cobbler ❧ Strawberry Shortcake ❧ The Best Bread Pudding ❧
Waterford Chocolate Mousse

Cassata Cake

THIS ITALIAN DESSERT tastes something like a cake version of cannoli.

2 pounds ricotta cheese (I use Sorrento's whole milk deli style)

1½ cups confectioners' sugar

1 teaspoon pure vanilla extract

¼ cup white crème de cacao

¼ cup small semisweet chocolate chips

2½ dozen plain ladyfingers, split

1½ cups heavy cream

⅓ cup granulated sugar

Maraschino cherries and walnuts or pecans, for decorating top of cake

Combine cheese, confectioners' sugar, vanilla, and crème de cacao in bowl of an electric mixer. Beat at medium speed for about 10 minutes; mixture should be fluffy. Stir in chocolate chips. Line bottom and sides of a 10-inch springform pan with ladyfingers. Pour in one third of filling; top with ladyfingers. Repeat layers, using remainder of filling and ladyfingers. Refrigerate overnight. When ready to serve, beat together cream and granulated sugar with a handheld electric mixer until stiff peaks form. Frost top of cake and decorate with cherries and nuts. Remove ring from springform pan.

SERVES 10

Eggnog Pudding

THIS RECIPE WAS USED *to tempt a friend of mine as a small child; otherwise she would not have received the nutritional benefits of milk. This is still her favorite pudding after all these years.*

¼ cup flour	1 tablespoon butter
1 tablespoon cornstarch	1 teaspoon pure vanilla extract
¾ cup sugar	2 egg whites, stiffly beaten
3 cups milk	Freshly grated nutmeg
2 egg yolks	

Mix together flour, cornstarch, and sugar in a saucepan; stir well. Add ½ cup of the milk to flour mixture and stir until smooth. In another saucepan, scald remaining 2½ cups milk (heat to just below boiling point); add to mixture. Cook and stir mixture over medium-low heat; do not allow to boil. In a bowl, beat egg yolks; remove ½ cup hot mixture and add to yolks to temper them; mix well and return to pot. Continue to cook over low heat for an additional 2 to 3 minutes. Remove from heat; add butter and vanilla. Thoroughly fold egg whites into the hot mixture. Place in individual custard dishes, sprinkle tops with nutmeg, chill, and serve. If you wish, you may serve this in a single bowl.

SERVES 6 TO 8

Grape-Nuts Pudding

THIS RECIPE WAS GIVEN to my friend Marge Maddox by an elderly little nurse in her seventies who never married. She would occasionally baby-sit for Marge's two young sons. One day, she brought this most wonderful dessert, a Maine specialty. You'll find this recipe to be not only yummy but easy.

2 cups milk	Dash of salt
2 eggs, beaten	1 cup Grape-Nuts cereal
½ cup sugar	Whipped cream or ice cream, for garnish
1 teaspoon pure vanilla extract	

Preheat oven to 350°F. Butter a 1½-quart baking dish.

Blend together milk, eggs, sugar, vanilla, and salt, using a handheld electric mixer. Pour into prepared dish. Sprinkle Grape-Nuts over top of custard and bake for 10 minutes. Give custard a couple of stirs to prevent cereal from sinking to bottom. Continue to bake for about 20 more minutes, or until a knife inserted in center comes out clean. Serve hot or cold with a dollop of sweetened whipped cream or ice cream.

SERVES 4 TO 6

Hazelnut Angel

1 large angel food cake	1 7-ounce Hershey's Symphony chocolate bar (almonds and toffee chips), broken into small pieces
½ cup sugar	
¼ teaspoon salt	
2 tablespoons cornstarch	½ cup raspberry preserves
1½ cups hazelnut coffee creamer	Whipped cream, for garnish
2 eggs, beaten	Fresh raspberries, for garnish
⅓ cup heavy cream, plus 1½ cups	Mint leaves, for garnish

Spray a 9-inch springform pan with cooking spray.

Tear cake into bite-sized pieces and place in a large bowl. Set aside. In a saucepan, stir together sugar, salt, and cornstarch until well blended. Slowly add hazelnut creamer to mixture, stirring well; add eggs. Cook over medium-low heat until thick, stirring constantly, 6 to 8 minutes. Remove from heat and stir in the 1/3 cup heavy cream. Pour 1 cup hot custard into a separate bowl; stir in chocolate pieces until melted. Set aside. Chill remaining custard completely. Whip the 1½ cups heavy cream until stiff, using a handheld electric mixer. Fold into chilled custard. Pour custard mixture over cake pieces, mixing well.

Put custard-cake mixture evenly into prepared pan. Spread custard-chocolate mixture evenly over the top of custard-cake mixture. Chill. Prepare final layer by melting preserves in microwave and spreading on top of custard-chocolate layer. Return to refrigerator until ready to serve. Remove springform ring and garnish with sweetened whipped cream, raspberries, and mint leaves.

SERVES 10 TO 12

Lemon Curd Pudding

THOSE OF YOU WHO *have visited our restaurant have probably noticed all the beautiful artwork on our walls. If you've never been here, imagine beautiful old walls painted a pale, pinky shrimp color covered with paintings of trailing ivy, pots of topiary trees filled with fresh vegetables, and the most handsome rooster I have ever seen.*

Bob Christian, along with his assistant, Mike Carnahan, is the man responsible for the ambiance in The Lady & Sons.

Recently, Bob and Mike were here in my home doing their special magic on the walls, while I was here working on this cookbook. Bob said he had a recipe he would like to share with me that was just out-of-this-world good. The next morning he brought it to me and thirty-five minutes later I was serving up the best *lemon dessert I had ever tasted.*

For a fabulous finish to your dinner party, serve this up in individual compotes with a dollop of fresh whipped cream, a sprig of fresh mint, and a lemon twist on top. You'll be a star with your guests, and you will have accomplished this with little or no sweat.

2 cups sugar	4 egg yolks
½ teaspoon salt	Juice and grated zest of 2 lemons
6 tablespoons all-purpose flour	4 egg whites, stiffly beaten
2 cups half-and-half	

Preheat oven to 350°F. Butter an 8 × 2-inch square pan.

Combine sugar, salt, and flour in a bowl, stirring well until all traces of flour have disappeared. Slowly stir in half-and-half; add egg yolks, lemon juice, and grated zest. Gently fold in egg whites. Pour into prepared pan. Set this pan inside a larger pan containing warm water 1-inch deep (this is baking in a water bath to prevent scorching). Bake for 30 to 35 minutes or until golden brown. This wonderful pudding will have a cake-like top with a rich, mouthwatering sauce on the bottom. Serve warm or cold.

SERVES 6 TO 8

Marvin's Banana Cream Pie

I DIDN'T HAVE THE HEART to tell him it was really banana pudding. If he wanted to call it Mama's Banana Cream Pie, so be it.

Savannah was about to be entertained that Saturday night by one of the greats, Marvin Hamlisch. But before he was scheduled to entertain us I wanted the opportunity for us to entertain him. So as he was lickin' the "banana cream pie" off his lips, I walked over to his table with one of our singing servers, Gabrielle Allen, and asked permission for her to sing a song for him.

He gave me a puzzled look and said, "What am I supposed to say, 'no'? And run the risk of not getting any more banana cream pie?"

Gabby burst into a beautiful rendition of Unforgettable. The entire restaurant hung on to every beautiful note.

Marvin held the greatest surprise for us: as Gabby finished her song, he immediately issued her an invitation to perform with him that night onstage. Looking at me, he said, "Mama, you have to be there, too." I can't tell y'all the excitement that Gabby felt and the pride I felt for her.

That night Gabby performed beautifully, captivating the audience while Marvin did his magic on the keyboard. Not only is he abundantly talented he is also a kind, warm and generous man with a fabulous sense of humor. Warm thanks to you, Marvin, from Savannah.

2 3-ounce boxes cook-and-serve vanilla pudding	1 8-ounce carton sour cream
2½ cups milk	1 12-ounce box vanilla wafers
4 tablespoons butter	6 to 8 bananas
1 teaspoon pure vanilla extract	TOPPING
1 cup heavy cream	2 cups heavy cream
½ cup sugar	½ cup sugar

Stir puddings into milk. Continue according to directions on box, using microwave or standard directions. Remove from heat and add butter and vanilla; allow to cool. Beat cream and sugar together until stiff peaks form, using a handheld electric mixer. Fold into cooled pudding. Stir in sour cream. Put a thin layer of custard in the bottom of a 10 × 3-inch square casserole dish, then line bottom and sides with vanilla wafers. Alternately layer with custard, cookies, and bananas, beginning and ending with custard.

For topping, beat cream and sugar together until stiff peaks form, using a handheld electric mixer. Frost pudding and refrigerate.

 You may choose to substitute instant pudding. I personally consider the cook-and-serve pudding second only to my homemade custards.

SERVES 18 TO 20

Not Yo' Mama's Banana Pudding

THIS RECIPE CAME TO ME *from my dear friend Rachel. She says it originally came to her from a fat friend, and since she has never trusted a skinny cook, she knew she had to try it. The recipe was originally named Mother's Banana Pudding, but Rachel knew it was too good to be* her *mama's pudding and felt she had to give it a more befittin' name.*

2 bags Pepperidge Farm Chessmen Cookies	1 14-ounce can sweetened condensed milk
6 to 8 bananas, sliced	1 12-ounce container frozen whipped topping, thawed, or an equal amount sweetened whipped cream
2 cups milk	
1 5-ounce box instant French vanilla pudding	
1 8-ounce package cream cheese, softened	

Line bottom of a 13 × 9 × 2-inch dish with 1 bag of cookies and put bananas on top. Blend milk with pudding mix well with a handheld electric mixer. Beat cream cheese and condensed milk together in a bowl until smooth; fold in whipped topping. Add to pudding mixture, stirring until well blended. Pour mixture over cookies and bananas; cover with remaining cookies. Refrigerate.

SERVES 12

The Lady & Sons' Peach Cobbler

It was an instant hit on the first day we offered this dessert at The Lady & Sons, and remains so today. This delicious cobbler can be found on our dessert trays at both lunch and dinnertime. It's so easy to make you won't believe it!

½ cup (1 stick) butter	cinnamon for sprinkling (optional)
1 cup sugar	
¾ cup self-rising flour	
¾ cup milk	
1 28-ounce can sliced peaches in heavy syrup, undrained (or use fresh if available; see note)	

Preheat oven to 350°F.

Place butter in oven in a 2-quart baking dish to melt. Stir sugar and flour together and mix well. Slowly add milk and continue to stir to prevent the batter from lumping. Being careful not to burn yourself, remove hot baking dish containing melted butter from oven; pour batter directly over butter in baking dish (DO NOT STIR). Spoon fruit on top of batter, then gently pour syrup on top (DO NOT STIR). Sprinkle with cinnamon, if using. The most important part of this dish is *not stirring* the mixture. Bake for 30 to 45 minutes or until golden brown. Your batter will rise above your fruit, producing the most wonderful of crusts. Serve warm with vanilla ice cream or fresh whipped cream.

If they are available by all means use fresh peaches. In a saucepan, mix two cups fresh peach slices with one cup sugar and one cup water. Bring to a boil, reduce heat, and simmer for 8 to 10 minutes, stirring occasionally. An almost equally good product is frozen peach slices. Simply follow the instructions for the fresh peach slices.

SERVES 8

Strawberry Shortcake

THIS ONE'S A KILLER, folks!

1 large angel food cake

CUSTARD

1 8-ounce package cream cheese, softened

1 14-ounce can sweetened condensed milk

1 12-ounce container frozen whipped topping, thawed

GLAZE

1 cup sugar

3 tablespoons cornstarch

3 tablespoons strawberry Jell-O

1 cup water

2 cups fresh strawberries, cut in half (if berries are extra large they may be cut into quarters)

Whole strawberries and mint leaves, for garnish

Slice cake, using a serrated-edge knife, horizontally into three equal layers. Mix together cream cheese, condensed milk, and whipped topping in a bowl; set aside. In a medium saucepan, stir together sugar, cornstarch, and Jell-O; add water. Cook, stirring over medium heat until thick. Remove from heat and allow to cool completely, then fold in strawberries. Place one layer of cake in a large clear bowl. Top with a layer of glaze, followed by a layer of custard mixture. Repeat layering in this order for remaining cake, glaze, and custard. For a pretty presentation, top cake with three whole fresh strawberries and fresh mint leaves.

SERVES 10 TO 12

The Best Bread Pudding

🌿

On September 20, 2000, Joanie Duke, one of the cutest little older ladies that I've had the pleasure of meeting bounded into the restaurant (and when I say "bounded in" I really mean it). She told me how much she enjoyed my recipes and that she had one of hers to share with me and shoved something into my hand, wrapped in plastic wrap. It was the best bread pudding I had ever wrapped my lips around. This quickly became the favorite bread pudding recipe for The Lady & Sons.

2 cups granulated sugar	SAUCE
5 large eggs, beaten	1 cup sugar
2 cups milk	½ cup (1 stick) butter, melted
2 teaspoons pure vanilla extract	1 egg, beaten
3 cups cubed Italian bread, cut and allowed to stale overnight in a bowl	2 teaspoons pure vanilla extract
	¼ cup brandy
1 cup packed light brown sugar	
¼ cup (½ stick) butter, softened	
1 cup chopped pecans	

Preheat oven to 350°F. Grease a 13 × 9 × 2-inch pan.

Mix together granulated sugar, eggs, and milk in a bowl; add vanilla. Pour over cubed bread and let sit for 10 minutes. In another bowl, mix and crumble together brown sugar, butter, and pecans. Pour bread mixture into prepared pan. Sprinkle brown sugar mixture over the top and bake for 35 to 45 minutes, or until set. Remove from oven.

For sauce, mix together granulated sugar, butter, egg, and vanilla in a saucepan. Over medium heat, stir together until sugar is melted. Add brandy, stirring well. Pour over bread pudding. Delicious served warm or cold.

🌿 *I've found sticking the bread in a 250°F oven for 10 to 15 minutes works just as well as staling the slices overnight.*

SERVES 8 TO 10

TOP: Paula's Loaded Oatmeal Cookies (pg 92), Chocolate Meringue Kisses (pg 85),
Cream Cheese Cookies (pg 87), Orange Brownies (pg 91), Cream Cheese Cookies (pg 87)

Mystery Mocha Cake (pg 46)

Blueberry Cream Cheese Tarts (pg 138)

Butter Pecan Cheesecake (pg 35)

Old South Jelly Roll Cake (pg 47)

Two Brothers' Chocolate Gobs (pg 100)

Eggnog Pudding (pg 106)

John Berendt's Favorite Angel Pie (pg 72)

Waterford Chocolate Mousse

THIS MOUSSE IS RICH and delicious. Serve in a beautiful crystal dish—Waterford recommended. Okay, maybe we don't have a piece of Waterford crystal. So, how about that beautiful glass dish that we all have, at one time or another, purchased from the dime store? You can also pour the mousse into individual compotes, and top with dollops of fresh whipped cream and strawberries.

6 4-ounce bars Ghirardelli bittersweet chocolate	1 cup sugar, plus ½ cup
⅔ cup extra-strong coffee (liquid)	2 cups heavy cream
4 large eggs, at room temperature, separated	

Break chocolate into smaller pieces; melt chocolate with coffee in top of double boiler. Using a fork, beat egg yolks slightly; stir in the 1 cup sugar and mix well. Add this mixture to melted chocolate and leave over heat, stirring until well blended and sugar is dissolved. Remove from heat and allow mixture to cool to the touch.

Using a handheld electric mixer, beat egg whites until stiff but not dry. Fold into chocolate mixture. Beat cream with the ½ cup sugar until soft peaks begin to form. Fold into chocolate mixture.

SERVES 12 TO 15

A Veil of Design
Over the City of Savannah

PAULA DEEN

THE SAVANNAH COLLEGE of Art and Design is a private, nonprofit, tax-exempt, accredited institution awarding Bachelor of Fine Arts, Master of Architecture, Master of Fine Arts, and Master of Arts degrees. Majors are offered in architectural history, architecture, art history, computer art, fashion, fibers, furniture design, graphic design, historic preservation, illustration, interior design, media and performing arts, metals and jewelry, painting, photography, product design, sequential art, and video/film. Now ain't all this just a mouthful!

The college was founded in 1978. Since its opening, the college has grown to occupy more than one million square feet in over forty buildings throughout Savannah's historic and Victorian district. The college's restoration of these old structures has helped preserve an important part of Savannah while providing the college with very possibly the most unique campus in the country.

In an unbelievably short time, SCAD has gained the reputation of being one of the finest art schools in the eastern United States. On a more personal level, my sons and I have had the pleasure of feeding guests of honor who are brought into our city by SCAD. We have many memories of meeting people from the world of the arts, such as Oscar de la Renta, Marvin Hamlisch, Bernie Casey, Bea Arthur, and others.

One such guest really sticks out in my mind: Danny Glover, the talented and gifted film star.

As soon as he and the other guests in his party were seated, I welcomed him to The Lady & Sons and told him that if there was anything I could do for him, "please don't hesitate to ask." He immediately had a request.

"May I please go back into the kitchen and visit the people preparing the food?" he asked. It was funny to see these two women, our head cook and her assistant, who are never at a loss for words (especially Nita), gaping at Danny Glover, unable to believe that he was in their kitchen.

I will never forget the consideration he showed to the people behind the scenes at The Lady & Sons. I think Mr. Glover and I both realize that the show cannot possibly go on without them.

So, thank you, Savannah College of Art and Design, for everything you've brought to our town, and for people who appreciate the arts and represent the humanities.

Candy

Almond Cups ❧ Chocolate Brickle ❧ Chocolate Cheese Fudge ❧

Chocolate Peppermint Patties ❧ Creamy Caramels ❧

English Toffee ❧ Miss Helen's Easter Eggs ❧ Mama's Divinity ❧

Peanut Clusters ❧ Penuche ❧ Pine Bark ❧ Almond Joy

Chocolate Balls ❧ Microwave Peanut Brittle ❧ Pralines ❧

Salty Dogs ❧ Uncle Bubba's Benne Candy ❧ Sugar 'n' Spice

Helpful Hints

1. To check a candy thermometer's accuracy, let it stand for about 10 minutes in boiling water (don't let it touch bottom of pan; clamp it on). The thermometer should read 212°F. If there is a variation, adjust by subtracting or adding the number of degrees of variation when testing candy.

2. Avoid making divinity or meringues on a humid or rainy day, as the increased moisture in the air will increase chances of failure.

3. Candy recipes traditionally indicate that candy is to be cooked to a certain stage, such as "soft ball," "thread," "hard crack," etc. The following table gives the temperatures and characteristics for the various stages:

Thread	230° to 234°F	Forms 2-inch ribbon as it falls from spoon
Soft ball	234° to 238°F	Rolls into soft ball and quickly loses its shape when removed from water
Medium ball	238° to 244°F	
Hard ball	244° to 254°F	Rolls into a firm but not hard ball; tends to flatten out soon after being removed from water
Very hard ball	254° to 265°F	Rolls into a hard ball and loses almost all its "plasticity"; rolls around on a plate after being removed from water
Light (soft) crack	265° to 285°F	Forms brittle threads that soften when candy is removed from water
Hard crack	290° to 300°F	Forms brittle threads that remain brittle after candy is removed from water
Caramelized sugar	310° to 338°F	Sugar melts and becomes golden brown; forms a hard brittle ball when dropped into cold water

4. For each cold water test, *always* use a fresh cupful of cold water. As the candy raises the water temperature, the water will be less accurate for each succeeding test. Spoon about ½ teaspoon of candy into cold water. Pick the candy out of the water with your fingers and roll it into a ball, if possible, so that you can determine the stage of the candy.

5. As you begin cooking, sugar crystals may form on the sides of the saucepan. Simply place a lid on pan for a couple of minutes. The moisture will help wash the crystals down. Insert candy thermometer and continue cooking per recipe instructions.

Almond Cups

1 8-ounce can Solo pure almond paste	Chocolate chips
2 eggs	Fresh pineapple slices
½ cup (1 stick) butter, melted, then cooled	Dried cherries or blueberries

Preheat oven to 350°F. Spray mini-muffin tins with nonstick cooking spray.

Place almond paste, eggs, and butter in a food processor and mix until well blended, smooth, and lump free. Fill muffin tins three quarters full with almond mixture. Top with chocolate chips, pineapple, or dried cherries or blueberries. Bake for 18 minutes or until golden.

YIELDS 24 CUPS

Chocolate Brickle

THIS QUICK AND DELICIOUS CANDY *will definitely satisfy that sweet tooth.*

1 cup (2 sticks) butter	1 teaspoon pure vanilla extract
1½ cups packed light brown sugar	1 12-ounce package semisweet chocolate chips
1½ cups mixed cocktail nuts (peanuts, almonds, cashews, etc.)	

Grease well a 13 × 9 × 2-inch baking pan and set aside.

Cook butter and sugar together in a heavy saucepan over medium heat for 5 minutes, stirring constantly with a wooden spoon. Add nuts and continue cooking and stirring for an additional 2 to 3 minutes. Remove from heat, add vanilla, and pour into baking dish. Sprinkle chocolate over top. As chocolate begins to melt, gently spread with a knife. Refrigerate for 20 to 30 minutes, until chocolate has set and candy is hard to the touch. You may cut into squares or invert pan, tapping on back with a wooden spoon to release candy, and break into pieces. Store in an airtight container, unrefrigerated.

YIELDS ABOUT 50 PIECES

Chocolate Cheese Fudge

THE AFTERNOON I FINISHED *testing this recipe, I took a plate of the fudge outside to the park to share with some of my lady friends. As they were oohing and aahing over the fudge, one of them said, "Oh, my goodness, Paula, it's wonderful."*

Her mouth dropped open after I told her the fudge was made with Velveeta cheese. "You're sh—ing me!" one of them said, which is not the language these ladies normally use! After all, this is the South.

I hope that when you serve it, you have as much fun as I did. This one is definitely a "Don't Miss!"

½ pound Velveeta cheese, sliced

1 cup (2 sticks) butter

1 teaspoon pure vanilla extract

1 cup chopped nuts

2 16-ounce boxes confectioners' sugar

½ cup cocoa

Spray lightly the bottom of a 9 × 2-inch square pan with a nonstick spray.

Over medium heat, in a saucepan, melt cheese and butter together, stirring constantly until smooth. Remove from heat. Add vanilla and nuts. In a large bowl, sift together sugar and cocoa. Pour cheese mixture into sugar-cocoa mixture, stirring until completely mixed. Candy will be very stiff. I have found it is easier to do the final mixing with my hands. Using your hands, remove candy from bowl and press evenly and firmly into pan. Because of the amount of butter in this recipe (which you *must* use), I like to pat the top of the candy with a paper towel to remove excess oil. At this point, you may want to refrigerate until firm, depending on how quickly you want to serve it. Thirty minutes will usually do the trick. Cut into squares.

For the most wonderful creamy, melt-in-your-mouth peanut butter fudge you'll ever eat, simply leave out cocoa and add 1 cup creamy peanut butter. Melt cheese and butter together, then add peanut butter and stir until smooth. Proceed as directed in original directions. I can never seem to make up my mind as to whether I want to add nuts. So, after placing the candy in the pan and patting out, I will usually sprinkle and press nuts onto top of half the pan of candy. That way, I've got the best of both worlds!

YIELDS ABOUT 36 SQUARES

Chocolate Peppermint Patties

2 16-ounce boxes confectioners' sugar	1 tablespoon pure peppermint extract
1 14-ounce can sweetened condensed milk	1 12-ounce package semisweet chocolate chips
½ cup (1 stick) butter, softened	½ bar paraffin

Mix together sugar, milk, butter, and peppermint in a large bowl. Roll mixture into small balls. Place on wax paper and chill. Melt chocolate chips and paraffin together in top of double boiler. Remove from heat, leaving chocolate over hot water. Using a toothpick, dip balls into melted chocolate. Cool on waxed paper.

YIELDS 75 TO 100 BALLS

Creamy Caramels

RICH AND DELICIOUS!

1 cup (2 sticks) butter	1 14-ounce can sweetened condensed milk
2¼ cups packed light brown sugar	1 teaspoon pure vanilla extract
⅛ teaspoon salt	
1 cup white Karo syrup	

Butter a 9 × 2-inch square pan.

In a heavy saucepan over medium heat, melt butter; stir in sugar and salt with a wooden spoon. Stir in syrup, followed by condensed milk. Using a candy thermometer, cook mixture to 245°F, stirring constantly. Remove from heat and stir in vanilla. Pour into prepared pan. While candy is cooling, cut waxed paper or plastic wrap in rectangular pieces. When candy is cooled you're ready to go! When cold, cut into candy-sized pieces (scissors may be easier to use than a knife) and wrap individually.

YIELDS ABOUT 100 PIECES

English Toffee

14 tablespoons (1 stick plus 6 tablespoons) butter	1 teaspoon pure vanilla extract
1 cup sugar	Dash of salt
2 tablespoons cold water	1 6-ounce bag semisweet chocolate chips or thin chocolate bars
½ cup chopped pecans	

Generously butter a cookie sheet.

Put butter, sugar, and water in a heavy pan or skillet over medium-high heat. Bring to a bubbling boil, stirring constantly with a wooden spoon, about 10 minutes. Add nuts to mixture, remove spoon from pan, and cook to a very brittle stage (300° to 310°F on a candy thermometer). Or, make a cold water test: candy will separate into hard, brittle threads. Remove from heat and add vanilla and salt. Pour onto prepared cookie sheet and spread to ¼-inch thickness. Cool slightly, top with chocolate chips or chocolate bars, and spread as it melts. Cool completely and break into pieces. Store in an airtight container.

YIELDS ABOUT 40 PIECES

Miss Helen's Easter Eggs

Potato candy is as intriguing to me as grits pies. Don't let the Easter Bunny come to your house without a basketful of these!

2 medium white potatoes	1½ teaspoons pure vanilla extract
½ cup (1 stick) butter, sliced	
2 16-ounce boxes confectioners' sugar	½ pound bitter chocolate bars

Boil potatoes in a small amount of salted water until soft. Drain and mash; measure out ½ cup into a bowl. Add butter to potatoes, blend well, and allow mixture to cool. Add sugar and vanilla to cooled potatoes (if your sugar is lumpy, you may want to sift it). Knead mixture by hand until smooth. Mold mixture into the shape and size of an egg. Repeat process until entire mixture has been molded. Refrigerate eggs for 1 hour.

Meanwhile, melt chocolate in a double boiler. Cool slightly, then, using a slotted spoon, dip eggs into chocolate, coating entire egg. Place on rack or baking sheet to drain, then transfer to waxed paper to harden.

Add any of the following to the mixture before molding, chilling, and dipping into chocolate:

Chocolate: Sift ¼ cup cocoa with the confectioners' sugar, then add to the mashed potato–butter mixture.

Nuts: Add ½ cup chopped nuts as you knead.

Fruit: Add ½ cup minced candied fruit or maraschino cherries and a few drops red food coloring as you knead.

Coconut: Add ½ cup flaked coconut as you knead.

Peanut Butter: Add chunky or creamy peanut butter to suit your taste as you knead.

YIELDS ABOUT 16 EGGS

Mama's Divinity

MY MOTHER made the most beautiful, wonderful divinity that I had ever seen. Forty-something years later, I can close my eyes and see this beautiful red-headed woman standing there twirling these heavenly mounds of candy onto the waxed paper. Remember not to make these candies on a rainy or humid day—they won't harden.

4 cups sugar	3 egg whites
1 cup white corn syrup	1 teaspoon pure vanilla extract
¾ cup cold water	1 cup chopped pecans

In a heavy saucepan over medium heat, stir together sugar, corn syrup, and water. Stir only until sugar has dissolved; do not stir after this point. Cook syrup mixture until it reaches 250°F on a candy thermometer, bringing it to the hard-ball stage.

While syrup is cooking, beat egg whites until stiff in the large bowl of an electric mixer. When candy reaches 250°F, carefully wrap the handle of the saucepan if necessary with a rag so you won't burn yourself and pour a slow, steady stream of syrup into the stiffly beaten egg whites, beating constantly at high speed. Add vanilla and continue to beat until mixture holds its shape. This could take up to 5 minutes. Stir in pecans.

Using 2 spoons, drop divinity onto waxed paper, using one spoon to push candy off the other. This may take a little practice because the technique is to twirl the pushing spoon, making the candy look like the top of a soft-serve ice cream. If candy becomes too stiff to twirl, add a few drops of hot water. You will need to work fast when making this type of candy. In fact, when it's time to twirl, it might not hurt to have a friend around.

YIELDS 50 TO 60 PIECES

Peanut Clusters

THIS IS ANOTHER YUMMY *quick and easy candy that will satisfy all chocoholics.*

1 pound white almond bark (available in supermarket baking section)	1 11.5-ounce bag Hershey's Milk Chocolate Chips
1 1-ounce square unsweetened chocolate (see note)	1 1-pound can salted cocktail peanuts
	1 teaspoon pure vanilla extract

Melt bark, chocolate, and chocolate chips together in an ovenproof baking dish (you may also use a double boiler or microwave). This can be done in the oven on low heat (250°F). Stir in peanuts and vanilla. Mix well. Drop by spoonfuls onto waxed paper.

Because the milk chocolate chips take longer to melt than the unsweetened chocolate and bark, you might want to begin melting them first. Heat in oven until half melted, then stir in the almond bark and unsweetened chocolate. Stir well and return to oven until mixture is melted.

YIELDS ABOUT 45 PIECES

Penuche

I DON'T KNOW if y'all have ever eaten those little candies called maple-nut goodies. I remember going as a child with Mama to Sears, Roebuck in Albany, Georgia. My mind would be set on the candy counter, and the first thing I'd do was look at Mama and collect my quarter, and off I'd go! One time I'd choose malted milk balls, and the next time I'd choose maple-nut goodies. The flavor of this penuche reminds me an awful lot of those smooth little bite-sized morsels.

1 16-ounce box light brown sugar	3 tablespoons butter
¾ cup milk	1 teaspoon pure vanilla extract
½ teaspoon salt	1 cup chopped nuts

Coat an 8 × 2-inch square pan with nonstick cooking spray.

Combine sugar, milk, and salt in a heavy 2-quart saucepan. Place over medium heat; stir only until sugar dissolves. When mixture comes to a boil, cook without stirring until it reaches soft-ball stage (236°F on a candy thermometer). Remove from heat; add butter, but do not stir. Cool to lukewarm. Add vanilla and beat, using a handheld electric mixer, until mixture begins to thicken. Stir in nuts and beat until thick. Pour at once into prepared pan. If candy is not hard enough, allow it to set in refrigerator until firm. Cut into squares.

YIELDS 36 SMALL SQUARES

Pine Bark

35 saltine crackers	6 1.5-ounce milk chocolate
1 cup (2 sticks) butter	Hershey Bars or 1 6.5-ounce
1 cup packed light brown sugar	package semisweet chocolate
½ teaspoon pure almond extract	chips

Preheat oven to 400°F. Line a 15 × 10 × 1-inch jelly roll pan with tin foil. Lightly spray foil with a nonstick cooking spray.

Place saltine crackers, salty side up, in prepared pan. In a saucepan, boil butter and sugar for 2 to 3 minutes, stirring constantly. Remove from heat; stir in almond. Pour over crackers and bake for 6 minutes. Remove from oven; top with candy bars or chocolate chips (I personally prefer the Hershey Bars). Spread chocolate evenly over crackers as it begins to melt. Cool slightly and transfer onto wax paper. Allow to cool completely.

YIELDS 35 SQUARES

Almond Joy Chocolate Balls

2 16-ounce boxes confectioners' sugar	1 14-ounce package shredded coconut
½ cup (1 stick) butter, softened	1½ cups chopped nuts
1 14-ounce can sweetened condensed milk	1 12-ounce package semisweet chocolate chips
1 teaspoon pure almond extract	½ bar paraffin

Cream together sugar and butter in a bowl; add milk. Stir in almond, coconut, and nuts; mix well. Form candy into 1-inch balls. Place on waxed paper and refrigerate at least 3 hours. Melt paraffin and chocolate in top of double boiler, stirring well. Remove from heat but allow chocolate to remain over hot water. (If chocolate becomes too thick, return to heat for a minute or so to thin.) With a toothpick, dip each ball in chocolate and place on waxed paper until set.

YIELDS 75 TO 100 BALLS

Microwave Peanut Brittle

YOU'LL NEVER MIND making peanut brittle again once you've used this recipe. From start to finish you're looking at ten minutes.

½ cup light corn syrup	1½ teaspoons butter
1 cup sugar	1 teaspoon pure vanilla extract
1½ cups salted peanuts (dry roasted)	1 teaspoon baking soda
¼ teaspoon salt	

In a microwavable, 2-quart dish, combine corn syrup and sugar; blend well. Cook in microwave on high for 4 minutes. Stir in nuts and salt, return to microwave, and cook for 4 more minutes on high. Add butter and vanilla; blend well. Cook for 1½ minutes on high. Remove from microwave and add baking soda, stirring until light and foamy. Pour onto a lightly greased cookie sheet or marble slab, spreading as thin as possible. Cool completely and break into pieces.

YIELDS ABOUT 36 PIECES

Pralines

THE FIRST TIME *I made this traditional southern candy I was exactly one month past my nine-teenth birthday. My precious forty-year-old daddy was undergoing open-heart surgery at Emory University in Atlanta, almost two hundred miles from our home.*

I'll never forget the day I got the call from Mama. "Paula, you can come see your daddy now. He's out of intensive care."

I knew I couldn't go see my daddy without a gift. And my gift to him was going to be a batch of homemade pralines.

Mother informed me that Daddy had had a light stroke during surgery, but the doctors were hoping for a full recovery. The setback did not stop Daddy from tearing into his box of pralines and gobbling them down.

Mother looked over at me and said, "Paula, is there any salt in these? Your daddy can't have any salt."

I said, "Yes, ma'am, there's a little salt in 'em," and immediately asked myself, what have you done to your daddy?

Well, that day Daddy ate his fill of these sweet morsels with no repercussions, but I'm so sad to say we lost this dear man four months later. Every time I make these wonderful candies I go back to the very first time I made and gave them to the most special of men: my daddy, Earl W. Hiers, who will forever remain young.

1½ cups granulated sugar	1 cup evaporated milk
1½ cups packed light brown sugar	2 tablespoons butter
⅛ teaspoon salt	1 teaspoon pure vanilla extract
3 tablespoons dark corn syrup	1½ to 2 cups pecan halves

Butter sides of a heavy 2-quart saucepan. Place sugars, salt, corn syrup, milk, and butter in saucepan. Over medium heat, stir constantly with a wooden spoon until sugars have dissolved and mixture comes to a boil. Continue to cook to a soft-ball stage (236°F on a candy thermometer), stirring occasionally. If you do a cold water test, ball of candy will flatten when you take it out of water. Remove from heat and allow to cool for 10 minutes. Add vanilla and nuts, and beat with a spoon by hand for about 2 minutes or until candy is slightly thick and begins to lose its gloss. Quickly drop by heaping tablespoons onto waxed paper. If candy should become too stiff to drop by spoon, repair by adding a few drops of hot water.

 You may prefer to drop these by the teaspoon, yielding you many more pieces. But the traditional southern praline is about 3½ inches in diameter.

YIELDS 9 TO 12 LARGE PRALINES

Salty Dogs

ONE OF THOSE *fun, messy, no-cooking recipes that's great for the children.*

1 12-ounce package butterscotch chips	½ bag caramel candies (see note)
1 cup marshmallow cream	2 tablespoons milk
½ cup nonfat instant powdered milk	2 cups salted cocktail peanuts, coarsely chopped
1 teaspoon pure vanilla extract	

Melt butterscotch chips in a glass bowl in a microwave on high for 2 minutes. Remove and stir in marshmallow cream and powdered milk. Add vanilla and stir well. Mixture will be very thick. At this point, I use my hands, kneading the mixture almost like I would bread dough. Roll a walnut-sized piece of the mixture into the shape of your little finger. Place on waxed paper to set.

Now here comes the messy part. Melt caramels and milk together in a glass dish in a microwave on high for 1½ to 2 minutes. Remove from microwave and stir well. Roll fingers in melted caramel, being careful that it's not so hot *these* fingers will burn *your* fingers. Roll immediately in chopped nuts, placing fingers back on waxed paper to harden. If you like, you may dip these in melted chocolate and you would swear you were eating a Baby Ruth!

 I use approximately ½ bag (22 pieces) of Brach's Milk Maid Rich and Creamy Caramels. You will be melting these caramels, and you will find your melted caramel will thicken as it cools, so you may find it necessary to pop it back in the microwave to loosen it up again. Or, you can sit the bowl of melted caramel over hot water to keep it at the right consistency. This would demand extra attention if children are making the candy.

YIELDS ABOUT 20 FINGERS

Uncle Bubba's Benne Candy

EVERY HOMETOWN has its heroes. In Savannah, one of our heroes started as a barefoot little boy running the streets of downtown Savannah, looking for music wherever he could find it. He is none other than the legendary Johnny Mercer.

His niece, Nancy Mercer Gerard, is my neighbor and dear friend. I just love it when Nancy starts talking about her "Uncle Bubba." Nancy was raised by her grandmother, Johnny's mother. Every year around November Grandma and Big Nancy, the family cook, began cooking the cakes and candies that were going to be shipped to Uncle Bubba. His work might not always allow him to come home for the holidays, but his mama made sure he had a piece of Savannah at Christmastime in that far-away place called Hollywood.

One of his two favorite things was benne seed candy. Nancy showed me how her grandmother did it.

In no time, she was finished with the candy. Wearing a big grin, she steady cut the candy and began to pass it around. Within a few seconds after popping the first bite into her mouth, she was squealing and laughing, "That's it! That's it! Just like I remember."

1 cup sesame seeds	½ cup milk
1 1-pound box light brown sugar	1 tablespoon white vinegar
2 tablespoons butter	

Butter an 11 × 8 × 2-inch Pyrex dish.

Wash sesame seeds and remove any sticks or stones that may be in the seeds. Drain well. Heat a cast-iron skillet over medium-high heat until a drop of water bounces around skillet. Pour seeds into hot skillet and stir constantly. Dry and parch seeds to a light brown, being careful not to burn. This will take about 2 minutes.

In a heavy saucepan, melt together sugar, butter, milk, and vinegar. Using a wooden spoon, stir constantly until ingredients are dissolved. Cook over medium to medium-high heat to light-crack stage. If you are using a candy thermometer, your desired temperature will be somewhere between 265° and 285°F. When Nancy was making the candy, she preferred the old-fashioned way of testing, which is to lift the wooden spoon out of the pot and allow a drop of candy to fall into a small amount of cold water. When the candy is ready, the drop will have a small thread on it when it hits the water. Remove from heat and beat in sesame seeds with your spoon. Pour immediately into prepared dish. Score while warm. Cut into squares when cool.

YIELDS ABOUT 24 PIECES

Sugar 'n' Spice

THIS RECIPE COMES FROM Pam Strickland, owner of River Street Sweets in Savannah. No Christmas table in the south is complete without Sugar 'n' Spice pecans.

¾ cup light corn syrup	2 teaspoons ground cinnamon
2 pounds sugar	3 pounds pecan halves
1 cup water	

Combine corn syrup, sugar, and water in a large heavy saucepan. Stir mixture only until sugar is completely moist. Place saucepan over medium heat and cook until mixture reaches 242°F. At that point, without stirring, immediately remove from heat and add cinnamon. Stir until mixture settles or stops boiling. Stir pecan halves into mixture all at once. Stir until all pecans are coated completely and begin to separate from each other and sugar crystallizes. When pecans are completely separated, pour them out onto a cookie sheet and allow them to cool.

YIELDS 3 POUNDS

Early Memories

JAMIE DEEN

SOME OF THE EARLIEST memories of my childhood, not surprisingly, revolve around food. My Great-Grandmother Paul was a true master of the southern vegetable.

Folks can sometimes take things for granted—especially children—but I tell you when we sat down to fried pork chops, fresh collards, homegrown snap beans with red potatoes, and vine-ripe tomatoes with just the right amount of salt and pepper, I *knew* it was something special. The food was so fresh you could almost smell the dirt. My thoughts at the time were that it might be the best food ever, and after growing up, I know that it *was* the best ever. Even better than Mom's.

My favorite candy that Mom made when I was growing up, hands down, was the buckeye. Though little more than a peanut butter ball dipped in chocolate the power of a buckeye was evident in the change of attitude in my teachers around the first of December. Just as April showers bring May flowers, the Christmas season brought homemade goodies from the Deen boys. Only the look my teachers got when I managed to sit still for ten minutes rivaled the excitement in their eyes when I walked in bearing the fruits of Mom's labors.

I really do remember the night power shifted to Bobby and me. Mom fried chicken in a cast-iron skillet on the stove from the time I had teeth up to today. My dad was always secure in the knowledge that he would have a breast of chicken at dinnertime. Moms always choose the thigh, so when I was five or six and sought the white meat myself, Dad was thankful chickens have a pair of breasts. Fast-forward three years and my brother has turned six himself and cast his eye toward one of the larger pieces. Dad never got more than a leg and two wings for the next fifteen years.

More Sweet Things

Banana Split Brownie Pizza ❧ Blueberry Cream Cheese Tarts ❧
Blueberry Dumplin's ❧ Captain Judy's Oreo Pineapple
Cream ❧ Charlotte Russe ❧ Cherry Torte ❧ Lemon Pineapple
Sherbet ❧ Chocolate Frost Ice Cream ❧ Clary's Apple
Blossom ❧ Cream Cheese Coffee Cake ❧ Easy Homemade
Oreo Ice Cream ❧ Fresh Apples with Butterscotch Dip ❧
Fresh Blackberry Crisp ❧ Fruit Slush ❧ Hot Mocha Float ❧
Mother's Nut Rolls

Banana Split Brownie Pizza

1 20-ounce box Duncan Hines Chewy Fudge Brownie Mix (plus ingredients to prepare)	2 bananas, sliced and tossed in lemon juice to prevent browning
1 8-ounce package cream cheese, softened	1 cup fresh strawberries, sliced
1 8-ounce can crushed pineapple, drained, juice reserved	1 cup chopped nuts
2 tablespoons sugar	Chocolate ice cream topping or chocolate syrup, for drizzling

Preheat oven to 350°F. Grease a 15-inch pizza pan.

Prepare brownie mix according to directions on box. Pour onto prepared pan. Bake for 20 minutes or until done. Remove from oven and cool. Beat cream cheese, pineapple, and sugar together in a bowl. Use any reserved pineapple juice at this time if needed to soften mixture to a good spreading consistency. Otherwise dispose of or save juice for another use. Spread mixture over brownie crust. Arrange banana and strawberry slices over cream cheese mixture. Sprinkle with chopped nuts and drizzle with chocolate ice cream topping. Refrigerate. To serve, slice as you would a pizza and enjoy!

SERVES 8 TO 10

Blueberry Cream Cheese Tarts

Don't forget this recipe for that last-minute emergency!

2 8-ounce packages cream cheese, softened	2 eggs
1 cup sugar	12 vanilla wafers
1 teaspoon pure vanilla extract	1 21-ounce can blueberry filling, or other pie filling

Preheat oven to 350°F. Place a paper cupcake liner in each cup of a muffin pan.

Beat cream cheese with a handheld electric mixer until fluffy. Add sugar and vanilla, beating well. Add eggs, one at a time, beating well after each addition. Lay a vanilla wafer, flat side down, in each muffin cup. Spoon cream cheese mixture over wafers. Bake for 20 minutes. Allow tarts to cool completely. Serve with blueberry filling on top, or pie filling of your choice.

YIELDS 12 TARTS

Blueberry Dumplin's

If you prefer blackberries over blueberries, by all means use them.

1 cup all-purpose flour	4 tablespoons milk
1 tablespoon sugar, plus 1½ cups	1 quart fresh or frozen blueberries
1 teaspoon baking powder	2 cups water
Pinch of salt	Vanilla ice cream or fresh cream, for serving
½ cup (1 stick) butter, softened	

Stir flour, the 1 tablespoon sugar, baking powder, and salt together in a bowl. Cut butter into dry ingredients, using a pastry cutter or fork. Add milk to form dough. Mix berries, the 1½ cups sugar, and water together in a saucepan and bring to a boil. Drop dumplings into hot boiling berries by the tablespoonful. Cover pot, reduce heat, and cook slowly for 20 to 30 minutes. Do not remove lid before 20 minutes has passed. Serve with vanilla ice cream or fresh cream.

SERVES 8

Captain Judy's Oreo Pineapple Cream

THE SPRING MORNING was purely made to order. Skimming across the Atlantic waters, we were on our way to a spot forty miles out, heading straight to the promise of a perfect fishing day.

My family and I take these fishing trips with only one captain. That would be none other than Captain Judy Helmey and her first mate—and also a licensed captain—Ali Young. If these two girls can't put you on the fish that must surely mean only one thing: all the fish have died.

If any of you are planning a vacation here in Savannah and would love the opportunity for a great day of deep-sea fishing, you can contact Judy at www.missjudycharters.com.

If you can't go fishing with her, at least try her favorite dessert. It's yummy, but not as yummy as her fishin'!

This is very pretty and easily feeds a crowd. To lighten the calorie load, you may use a reduced-fat Oreo cookie and/or Cool Whip whipped topping. If you decide to use Cool Whip, you will need the 16-ounce container.

1 1-pound package Oreo cookies	1 20-ounce can crushed pineapple
1½ cups sugar	¼ cup (½ stick) butter
2 tablespoons all-purpose flour	1 16-ounce jar maraschino
1 cup heavy cream, plus 3 cups	cherries halves

Crush Oreos. (Now, Captain Judy says she does this using a fish rag. When I asked her what the hell a "fish rag" was, she said, "It's just one of those rags we use when we go fishing." Well, I personally found the food processor worked pretty good for me.) Set aside. In a saucepan, stir together one cup of sugar and flour. Add the 1 cup heavy cream; blend well. Add pineapple, including juice, to cream mixture. Place over medium heat. Cook mixture until it begins to thicken, stirring constantly. Remove from heat and add butter. Allow to cool completely. The mixture will cool faster if you transfer it from hot saucepan to a bowl. Beat the 3 cups heavy cream with a handheld electric mixer until soft peaks form; slowly add remaining sugar and continue to beat until fairly stiff peaks form. In a 10-inch glass bowl, layer Oreos, pineapple mixture, whipping cream, and cherries in that order, being sure to tuck some cherries around sides.

SERVES 15 TO 20

Charlotte Russe

My friend, cookbook author Damon Fowler, is a wealth of information when it comes to the history of southern dishes, so I hope you enjoy preparing and partaking of the dish as well as the history lesson he has given us.

Charlotte Russe is supposed to have been invented by the great French chef Antonin Carême, whose heyday was the first quarter of the nineteenth century. By the second quarter of the same century, this dessert had already become a popular standard in English and American cookery, especially in the South. Some southern cookbooks had as many as a half dozen variations. This one returns to the early cream and beaten egg white formula for the filling. You may vary it by folding in different flavorings, crushed fruit, or a few spoonfuls of fruit preserves.

1 tablespoon unflavored gelatin	2 tablespoons sweet sherry (don't use cooking sherry)
¼ cup milk	
3 cups heavy cream	½ cup fruit preserves (optional)
1¼ cups sugar	7 large egg whites
1 tablespoon homemade vanilla extract or 1 teaspoon pure vanilla extract	Fresh berries or cut fruit, for garnish
Homemade angel food cake or ladyfingers	

Soften gelatin in a tablespoon or so of cold water in a bowl. If milk is cold, heat it very briefly—just enough to bring it to room temperature—and completely dissolve gelatin in it. Let it sit while you prepare rest of filling, stirring it every now and again to keep gelatin from separating and settling to bottom.

Sweeten 2 cups of the cream with 1 cup of the sugar and beat it with a handheld electric mixer until it is fairly stiff. Add vanilla and fold it in. Stir in dissolved gelatin and gently but thoroughly fold it into whipped cream and set it aside.

Cut cake into ladyfinger-sized pieces, about ½ inch thick by 1 inch in width and as long as your mold is deep. Line bottom and sides of a 3-quart mold or bowl with cake, being sure that there are no gaps in it. Hold back enough of cake to cover top of mold or bowl. Sprinkle cake with sherry and spread it with a thin layer of jam or fruit preserves, if using.

Beat egg whites to stiff but not dry peaks with a handheld electric mixer, then fold thoroughly into whipped cream and gelatin filling. Spoon filling into cake-lined mold, making sure there are no gaps or air pockets between filling and cake. Press reserved cake on top of filling.

Chill until cream is set, 4 to 6 hours. When you are ready to serve, gently run a knife around edges of mold to make sure that the Charlotte has not stuck to it, then invert onto plate. Carefully lift off mold.

Lightly sweeten remaining 1 cup cream with remaining ¼ cup sugar and beat until it is stiff. If you like, you can put it into a pastry bag and pipe it onto the Charlotte, or simply spoon it on, using it to cover any gaps or splits in outer layer of cake. Garnish with fresh fruit.

SERVES 6 TO 8

Cherry Torte

THIS IS REALLY, REALLY GOOD. *The saltiness from the crackers and the sweetness of the cherries is a great flavor combination.*

6 egg whites, at room temperature	1½ cups chopped nuts
¾ teaspoon cream of tartar	1 2.6-ounce container Dream Whip
2 teaspoons pure vanilla extract	
2 cups sugar	2 21-ounce cans cherry pie filling
2 cups broken saltine crackers	

Preheat oven to 350°F. Generously grease a 13 × 9 × 2-inch baking pan.

In a large bowl, mix egg whites, cream of tartar, and vanilla. Beat with a handheld electric mixer until light and foamy. Slowly add sugar and continue to beat until stiff. Fold crackers and nuts into meringue. Pour mixture into prepared pan. Bake for 30 minutes. Remove from oven. Prepare Dream Whip according to package and spread onto cooled torte, spooning cherry filling on top.

SERVES 15

Lemon Pineapple Sherbet

This wonderful recipe came from Kentucky around the turn of the last century.

2 quarts whole milk	2 cups sugar
1 14-ounce can sweetened condensed milk	1 cup fresh lemon juice (from about 6 lemons)
1 20-ounce can crushed pineapple with juice	

Mix together all the ingredients, stirring until well blended. When you add lemon juice, the sherbet will appear to curdle, but that is not a problem. Pour into an electric ice cream maker. Freeze according to manufacturer's instructions.

SERVES 8 TO 10

Chocolate Frost Ice Cream

This is real good, and it tastes much like those Frosties you get from Wendy's.

1 14-ounce can sweetened condensed milk	1 gallon chocolate milk
1 tablespoon pure vanilla extract	1 12-ounce container whipped topping

Mix together all ingredients. You will need to churn this in 2 batches. Fill ice cream maker two-thirds full, freeze, and repeat process with remaining liquid.

SERVES 16 TO 20

Clary's Apple Blossom

MY DEAR FRIEND *Paulette Faber is the epitome of a true Southern Belle. She and her husband, Michael Faber, are the owners of Clary's Café, located at 404 Abercorn Street in the historic section of Savannah. Paulette's childhood memories of Clary's are of a landmark for the locals. Dr. Clary, she remembers, had on one side of his store a pharmacy and on the other side of the store a soda fountain and lunch counter. No one could ever come into Clary's without going to the soda fountain for a vanilla Coke, malt, banana split, or ice cream cone. As locals lingered over these treats, you could always count on a lot of laughter and neighborhood gossip.*

If you have read Midnight in the Garden of Good and Evil *by John Berendt, you will know that Clary's was a hangout for so many of the interesting characters that are depicted in this story.*

Michael and Paulette have asked me to extend a personal invitation to y'all to drop in and visit Clary's the next time you're in Savannah. Along with this invitation comes the recipe to one of Clary's most often ordered desserts. Paulette says one shell may serve two people, depending on how well your guests know each other.

1 package small flour tortillas (6 inches in diameter)	Vanilla ice cream
1 21-ounce can apple pie apples, warmed	1 19-ounce jar Smucker's Special Recipe Butterscotch Caramel ice cream sauce

You will need to fry tortillas individually into the shape of a taco salad shell. To do this, heat enough oil in a large deep pot, being sure that oil is deep enough to accommodate shell. Place a flat tortilla in hot oil. Using a ladle, immediately press center of tortilla down, holding it until tortilla is set into shape of a shell. Continue to fry until golden brown. Drain each fried shell upside down on paper towels to remove excess oil. Repeat this process for as many servings as you will need, allowing 1 shell per person. This step can be done early in the day.

Just before serving, place a layer of warm apples in bottom of each shell. Scoop ice cream over apples and drizzle caramel sauce over top.

SERVES 4 TO 6

Cream Cheese Coffee Cake

DOUGH

1 cup sour cream

½ cup granulated sugar

½ cup (1 stick) butter

1 teaspoon salt

2 packages active dry yeast

½ cup warm water (110° to 115°F)

2 eggs, beaten

4 cups all-purpose flour

FILLING

2 8-ounce packages cream cheese, softened

¾ cup granulated sugar

1 egg, beaten

2 teaspoons pure vanilla extract

⅛ teaspoon salt

GLAZE

2½ cups confectioners' sugar

¼ cup milk

1 teaspoon pure vanilla extract

Toasted sliced almonds (optional)

In a saucepan, combine sour cream, granulated sugar, butter, and salt. Cook over medium-low heat, stirring constantly, for 5 to 10 minutes, or until well blended. Cool to room temperature. In a mixing bowl, dissolve yeast in water. Add sour cream mixture and eggs; mix well. Gradually stir in flour (dough will be very soft). Divide into 4 equal balls; cover and refrigerate overnight.

For filling, beat together cream cheese and sugar with a handheld electric mixer. Add egg, vanilla, and salt and mix well.

Grease 2 baking sheets. Remove dough from refrigerator and knead each ball 5 to 6 times on a floured surface. Roll each portion into a 9 × 12-inch rectangle. Spread one quarter of filling on each rectangle to within 1 inch of edges. Roll up jelly roll style from long side; pinch seams and ends to seal. Place seam side down on prepared baking sheet (2 rolls to a sheet, as they will spread). Cut 6 X's on top of each loaf. Cover and let rise until nearly doubled, about 1 hour. Preheat oven to 375°F. Bake for 20 to 25 minutes or until golden brown.

For glaze, combine confectioners' sugar, milk, and vanilla and drizzle over loaves. Sprinkle with almonds, if using. Store in refrigerator. Freezes well.

YIELDS 4 LOAVES

Easy Homemade
Oreo Ice Cream

No CHURN IS NEEDED *for this tasty ice cream.*

3 egg yolks (see note)

1 14-ounce can condensed milk

4 teaspoons pure vanilla extract

1 cup coarsely crushed Oreo cookies
(about 12 cookies)

2 cups heavy cream, whipped
(do not use whipped topping
or Cool Whip)

In a large bowl, beat egg yolks; stir in condensed milk and vanilla. Fold in cookies and whipped cream. Pour into aluminum foil–lined 9 × 5-inch loaf pan or other 2-quart container. Cover and freeze 6 hours or until firm. Scoop ice cream from pan or peel off foil and cut into slices. Freeze leftovers.

🌿 *Eating raw eggs carries the risk of salmonella. Foods containing raw eggs should not be consumed by the very young, the very old, pregnant women, or anyone with a compromised immune system.*

SERVES 8

Fresh Apples with Butterscotch Dip

THIS IS NICE at Christmastime.

2 12-ounce packages butterscotch morsels	1 tablespoon cinnamon
2 14-ounce cans sweetened condensed milk	1 tablespoon pure vanilla extract
2 tablespoons butter	3 red apples, unpeeled
2 tablespoons white vinegar	3 green apples, unpeeled
	½ cup lemon juice

Put butterscotch morsels, condensed milk, butter, vinegar, cinnamon, and vanilla in a heavy saucepan. Cook over medium-low heat, stirring constantly until smooth and hot. Cut each apple into 8 wedges, and toss in lemon juice to prevent apples from turning brown. Place apples on a serving dish, alternating green and red apples around the dish. Fill a small chafing dish with butterscotch dip and place in center. Garnish with fresh mint leaves around apples. You may substitute peanut butter morsels for butterscotch.

YIELDS 48 WEDGES

Fresh Blackberry Crisp

4 cups fresh blackberries, or frozen blackberries, thawed and drained well	1 cup all-purpose flour
	¼ cup (½ stick) butter, at room temperature
2 cups sugar	Vanilla ice cream or sweetened whipped cream, for serving
½ teaspoon cinnamon	

Preheat oven to 350°F. Butter sides and bottom of a 9 × 2-inch square pan.

Put blackberries in a bowl, sprinkle with 1 cup of the sugar, add cinnamon, and mix well. In a separate bowl, stir together flour and remaining 1 cup sugar. Using a fork or pastry cutter, cut butter into flour until crumbly. Pour sugared berries into prepared pan, and cover with flour mixture. Bake for 45 to 50 minutes. Serve with vanilla ice cream or a dollop of sweetened whipped cream.

SERVES 8

Fruit Slush

THIS IS A WONDERFUL *breakfast dessert.*

1½ cups sugar	1 20-ounce can crushed pineapple with juice
2 cups hot water	
1 6-ounce can orange juice concentrate, plus 3 cans water	6 bananas, mashed
	1 12-ounce package frozen sliced strawberries, thawed (enough so they can be separated)
1 23-ounce can or bottle apricot nectar	

Mix sugar and hot water together and stir until sugar is dissolved. Stir in remaining ingredients. Pour into small containers and freeze (plastic cups will work well). When this breakfast dessert is removed from freezer, it will thaw rather quickly.

SERVES ABOUT 12

Hot Mocha Float

A WONDERFUL FINALE to any meal on a cold winter day!

½ cup sugar	1 quart milk
½ cup cocoa	2 cups water
3 tablespoons instant coffee granules	½ pint vanilla ice cream

About 20 minutes before serving, in a large saucepan with wire whisk or spoon, stir together sugar, cocoa, and coffee. Over medium heat, slowly add milk and water until well blended. Heat until mixture is hot, but not boiling, stirring occasionally. Remove from heat. Ladle into six 8-ounce mugs. Top each with spoonful of ice cream.

SERVES 6

Mother's Nut Rolls

DOUGH

5 cups all-purpose flour

3 tablespoons sugar

½ teaspoon salt

1 cup (2 sticks) butter, softened

2 ¼-ounce packages dry yeast

1 cup sour cream

4 egg yolks

FILLING

4 egg whites

2½ pounds ground walnuts

1 cup sugar

GLAZE

1 egg, beaten

1 tablespoon water

Stir together flour, sugar, and salt in a bowl; cut in butter until mixture resembles cornmeal. In another bowl, prepare yeast according to package directions. Add sour cream and egg yolks to yeast. Blend sour cream mixture into flour mixture. Make 8 balls of dough; on a lightly floured surface, knead each ball of dough until dough is smooth but not too sticky. Cover dough and place in refrigerator overnight.

Take dough from refrigerator about 20 minutes before using. If last balls of dough become too soft, return them to refrigerator; take one out at a time. Roll dough out on granulated sugar to a 12 × 9-inch rectangle.

For filling, beat egg whites with a handheld electric mixer until frothy; add nuts and sugar. Mix well.

Spread filling over dough. Cut dough into 3 strips; roll each strip as for a jelly roll. Cut each strip crosswise into little rolls. Depending on size of each roll, you should be able to get 15 to 18 rolls from each ball.

Preheat oven to 350°F. Grease a cookie sheet; place rolls seam side down on sheet. For glaze, combine egg and water and brush over each roll. Bake for 20 to 25 minutes, until light to medium brown. Remove from oven; cool for 2 to 3 minutes and remove carefully to wire rack to cool completely. These freeze very well.

YIELDS 120 TO 144 ROLLS

Metric Equivalencies

LIQUID AND DRY MEASURE EQUIVALENCIES

CUSTOMARY	METRIC
¼ teaspoon	1.25 milliliters
½ teaspoon	2.5 milliliters
1 teaspoon	5 milliliters
1 tablespoon	15 milliliters
1 fluid ounce	30 milliliters
¼ cup	60 milliliters
⅓ cup	80 milliliters
½ cup	120 milliliters
1 cup	240 milliliters
1 pint *(2 cups)*	480 milliliters
1 quart *(4 cups, 32 ounces)*	960 milliliters *(.96 liter)*
1 gallon	3.84 liters
1 ounce *(by weight)*	28 grams
¼ pound *(4 ounces)*	114 grams
1 pound *(16 ounces)*	454 grams
2.2 pounds	1 kilogram *(1,000 grams)*

Index